THE EAST IS EAST,
AND
THE WEST IS WEST.
OR, IS IT?

THE EAST IS EAST, AND THE WEST IS WEST. OR, IS IT?

✦

A Non-Academic Approach to DIVERSITY 101

Gene J. Cho

iUniverse, Inc.
New York Bloomington Shanghai

THE EAST IS EAST, AND THE WEST IS WEST. OR, IS IT?
A Non-Academic Approach to DIVERSITY 101

iUniverse books may be ordered through booksellers or by contacting:

iUniverse
1663 Liberty Drive
Bloomington, IN 47403
www.iuniverse.com
1-800-Authors (1-800-288-4677)

Because of the dynamic nature of the Internet, any Web addresses or links contained in this book may have changed since publication and may no longer be valid.

The views expressed in this work are solely those of the author and do not necessarily reflect the views of the publisher, and the publisher hereby disclaims any responsibility for them.

ISBN: 978-0-595-47443-1 (pbk)
ISBN: 978-0-595-91720-4 (ebk)

Printed in the United States of America

Contents

Preface

From 1990 until 1994, I was an occasional contributor of articles to the Flower Mound (Texas) weekly paper *Pipeline*, published by Ms. Doe Royal who also was the chief editor. She was active in Mayflower Congregational Church, a soprano in the choir, and I was the minister of music at the church. During these years as fellow church members, our friendship grew, and it was Doe who had suggested that I write for her paper. Many of the articles contained in this little publication originally appeared in *Pipeline*, under the series entitled "*The East is East, and the West is West. Or is it?*" My contribution to the series came to an abrupt end in 1994 when I took up a two-year visiting professor appointment in Hong Kong.

A few years ago I found the clippings of these articles in a pile of old papers. In rereading them, I found that the same themes written some fifteen years ago still ring true. Still, I felt I should have these very personal narratives validated by unbiased third parties, that these articles still contain points of interest for today's general readership. So I sent several articles to a few friends of *long* standing who had not read them before, among them Ms. Winnie Chow (Los Altos, CA), a close friend from college days back in Taiwan, who also was the leading soprano in the glee club that I founded *half a century* ago. I was delighted that they regarded many of these stories and my personal reminiscences both entertaining and enlightening, even "educational," as a few had mentioned. And I was particularly gratified by their unanimous suggestion that I should seek publication of these articles as a book, for "leisure reading" during the summer days or winter holidays.

While the essence of most of these original newspaper articles and even the time references in the narratives were left unaltered, I have edited and lengthened some and rewritten a few others, as a way of making the this publication more current. I also added a few new articles to supplement certain aspects and perspectives of the "East *versus* West" stories that I felt needed fuller treatment.

All the stories herein are from the author's personal encounters. Among them are the tales told to him by his maternal grandmother, parents and close relatives, stories from their own life's more memorable experiences. And all the subjective perspectives are my own. The general tenor of the narratives is not serious and certainly not scholarly. And the readers would forgive me if I slip from time to time into wandering thoughts and aimless ramblings, where there is no demarcation between the sacred and profane. But the story is always told in candor and occasionally with humor. For I believe that truth—even subjective truth and harsh reality of life—can be made a little more palatable when it is told with a "spoonful" of lampoon.

This is a personal journal. It is in these pages that the author feels free and un-beholden to anyone to record life's encounters, impressions and opinions just as he saw them. And he hopes, through this small publication, to let others look into his mind and heart.

I dedicate this book to my children Jocelyn and Geoffrey. For I believe deep in my heart that they will cherish and regard these encounters in their father's life as an undeniable part of their own family and cultural legacy.

GJC
Fall 2007
Denton, Texas

Introduction (The Author's Self-Introduction)

Nearly every person possesses a measure of self-identity, a sense of belonging that has been nurtured over the years and by many things such as the place of birth, the parents and siblings, local customs, school friends and, of course, the language or even the peculiar strain of local accent. I always have admired people who exhibit a clear sense of self-identity, whether in deeds or words. This was perhaps because I had never had a strong sense of self-identity, but only a vague idea about whom or what I really was.

I was born in Taiwan, and that would automatically classify me as a Chinese. But, actually, I was born a Japanese, because Taiwan was then a part of Imperial Japan, and Taiwan belonged to the Japanese archipelago, although, granted, a bit far off from the four main islands of Japan. My first language was Japanese, and I did not know a word of Chinese or any other language or dialect until I was about ten years old. After the war I began to learn to speak *holo*—an archaic dialect from northern China still spoken by the majority of native Taiwanese—and, only after that, Mandarin, the official language of China that is now commonly called *putong-hua*, meaning 'common tongue.'

After graduating from college in Taiwan, I came to the States and, for nearly five decades, have been speaking English almost exclusively. Today, my Chinese or even Japanese—my 'mother tongue,' so to speak—is laughably awkward, so much so that my wife tells me that I dream in English, that my Mandarin sounds more like American missionaries trying to negotiate Chinese.

The truth is, I really couldn't tell you in what language I do my thinking or dreaming. It is all sort of jumbled up. I also had never lived in one place longer than six years. That is, until I came to Texas. My family moved out of a small mining town when I was about six years old, and we moved again when I was in the seventh grade. Since I attended an all-Japanese primary school, I now don't have any primary-school classmates still living in Taiwan (except one). For all the Japanese who lived in Taiwan were shipped back to Japan soon after the war ended. During my junior and senior years, I changed school three times, and this transiency during those impressionable years did not allow me time to sufficiently cultivate lasting friendship with any of my classmates. I attended a university far from home (Hualien), on the "other side" of the Island, and could not say with any certainty that I had lived at home for any appreciable length of time since graduating from high school.

Soon after graduating from Chung Hsing National University, I came to America. By July 2008, I have lived in the United States for half a century! And, more than anywhere in the world, I feel at home in Texas, even without the cowboy boots and ten-gallon hat, or a gunrack on the back of my pickup truck. I feel perfectly at home here and, I am sure, have unconsciously assumed many local mannerisms (except the "Texas drawl" accent!). Occasionally, my Chinese friends and American colleagues at the university and fellow church members would tell me that I don't "act or speak like an *average regular* Chinese." My son tells me that I am more like a Japanese, while my wife occasionally calls me her *Chinese-American* husband, especially when she gets a bit annoyed if I fail to immediately understand what she is saying in Mandarin. (I really don't think she meant that she has a *real* Chinese husband, but I never asked.)

I can still remember that, during those schooling years, I had a problem of focusing, because there were too many subjects that I liked. I liked reading and writing, math, science, arts and music, history, and geography. I even liked sports and, although my father regarded me as somewhat awkward, I became fairly good at a few events. But, of all the school subjects, I excelled in the arts, music in particular.

However, in those postwar years when life was hard and a career opportunity was limited, music and arts were considered a luxury and 'sissy' subjects, and no boys with any degree of self-respect would consider pursuing music as a life career. So, in order to honor my parents' wishes, I entered Chung Hsing University with a major in agricultural economics, because my parents had some agricultural lands and they wanted their eldest son to manage the family estates. After graduation, however, I asked my parents for permission to study music in America. By that time, they no longer possessed any of the lands they had acquired, literally with their labor of sweat of many years, due to the Taiwanese government's sweeping land reform under the "land for the tiller" policy. Also, my parents had already suspected that I had little interest in more practical things in life and in pursuing a lucrative career. Since my father was a Christian minister, they figured that majoring in music might be a way for their son to follow in the footsteps of his father, even only after a fashion—to become a "music minister," perhaps in the United States. (There was no full-time music ministry career in Taiwan.)

I came to the United States and, after five years, managed to earn two graduate degrees in church music. But, while serving as part-time choir director at several churches during graduate school and seminary years, I also discovered that many ministers were nearly tone-deaf, that they were really more interested in having the kind of music in their church that would arouse the congregation, make them 'feel good' and thereby more inclined to reach deeper into their pocket(-book)s. That, unfortunately, was not my ideal of the role of music in the church. My ideal may very well have even been impractical, unrealistic and "off target" (which is the original meaning of the Aramaic/Hebrew word "sin"). At any rate, I had at least discovered that *church* music was not for me. So I decided to pursue a career in music teaching, and got my first full-time teaching position in Detroit. It was there that I knew I finally found my life's calling, a *niche* in the real world.

In hindsight, it seemed that all the past leading up to that first full-time position had been a preparation for this unexpected calling: studies in science, mathematics, history, art, experience as conductor of the university's glee club (which I founded), and graduate training in composition, voice, conducting, and theology during the seminary years. Today, I sometimes look back and find it hard to believe that I have been teaching *music theory* for about four decades—five years between Chicago and Detroit, and over three and a half decades in Denton, Texas—and have enjoyed every bit of it. I feel grateful.

In looking back, I also would remember that there were times when I lamented that I did not have a more stable childhood, that I did not have a more focused area of interest. And although I could claim proficiency in several academic disciplines, and could speak three or four languages fluently, I am not particularly masterful in one area or eloquent in one particular language.

Since coming to Texas, however, I also have come to a new realization that there is actually one unique advantage in NOT having a strong sense of self-identity: it is a vantage point to observe and assess things and people nearly totally objectively, without any abiding preconception or strong persuasion to one particular point of view. For the absence of affinity to one nationality, lack of a strong conviction to one religious (that is, doctrinal) belief, or one philosophical stance or political persuasion, or an all-consuming allegiance to one cultural heritage, allows me to look at life and all its manifestations more objectively, honestly, and wholly unencumbered. I even entertain the thought that perhaps I am more impartial than many first-generation Asians living in America and, therefore, more able to see and understand why Asians are how they are. And since I have spent nearly all of my adult years in the United States, more often than not in the surroundings where there were but a few Asians, or none at all, I am able to observe objectively and to understand why Americans are how they are. For me, life in America has been an endlessly fascinating learning experience, far more so than any "multicultural" and "diversity" classes a university could ever offer me in the study of human society.

And it is from this experience and my somewhat unique vantage point that the question of "The East is east, and the West is west. Or is it?" has begun to emerge in my mind for many years. In this sense, this little book is a term paper of my study in the life's perspectives of "East *versus* West."

This is a series of highly personal narratives, full of subjective viewpoints and interpretation of facts and encounters, mixed with remembrances, anecdotes, folk legends and historical tales. This little book is a collection of reflections on scenes I have watched through the periscope of my own eyes and mind. I would therefore beg the kind understanding and indulgence from you (the kind readers,) to accommodate the author's highly personal and, to be sure, peculiar perspectives of life and interpretation of *his* life's experiences. There are passages in this book that, I am sure, would appear satirical to some readers, or even sacrilegious to others. But they are all candid, honest, and sincere. And if any of these stories brings you the readers a nod, a smile, or a thought that leads you to further reflection—I dare not say contemplation—then I shall be more than richly and abundantly rewarded.

Instead of a quickstep through life's pathways, I like to linger a while from time to time, here and there, to smell the roses, as it were, and lose myself in daydreaming. I find that, in spite of all the societal woes and human miseries around us, there is still so much wonder and mystery in life and in the world. When we lift our eyes, we will see that there are wonders and beauties in sunshine and twinkling lights in the dark void above us, and when we stop our hurried gaits, we can still feel our heart rejoicing in the soft breezes and marveling at the blinding lightning. And when human hatred seems so fearfully ugly and dreadfully intense, we can quietly look around and find comfort in renewal of faith in the human race, that there are still innocent smiles, kind gestures, and helping hands in the many corners of the back streets and rural roads.

I like recalling the opening phrase from an old Japanese literary work called *Tsure-na-Gusa* (or, some would pronounce it as *Tsure-zure Gusa*), "*Grasses [along the] Pathway [of life]*," which reads as follows (loosely translated):

> *Hana wa sakari ni, tsuki wa kuma naku*
> *o nomi miru mono kawa?*
> (Shall I look at the flower only when it is in full blossom,
> or at the moon only when it is full and without shadow?)

Life has both lighted and shaded phases, and one without the other would not a full and vibrant life make. Humankind has its east and west, and one without the other would not a colorful and dynamic human race make. While we may never be fluent in many of the Eastern and Western tongues, or fully understand the thoughts of man and woman, we could be much better and the world more harmonious if we would accept the fact that we are all alike and unalike one another, and that we could not be truly ourselves without the other. And the kingdom of God will come to this earth only when we truly believe that we are all created equal, even if slightly differently, by the same pair of all-wise and almighty hands. As our wise forbearers have affirmed, in that most powerful statement, in the *Declaration of Independence*:

THIS IS TRUE AND SELF-EVIDENT,

AND IS OUR UNALIENABLE RIGHTS

1

The East Is East, and The West Is West. Or Is It?

A little over five centuries ago, Columbus was finally granted the support of Queen Isabella of Spain for his daring venture to reach the mysterious *East*, by way of a *western* route, sailing across the unimaginably vast and wholly uncharted ocean. Two centuries earlier still, another Genoese, Marco Polo, in the company of his father and uncle, had succeeded eventually in traversing the whole length of the northern Silk Roads to reach India and then the Land of *Cathay* (that is, China), over the eastern route across the vast stretch of land and through the impossibly treacherous mountainous passages. For some time now, the Italians—Venetians and Genoese in particular—as well as Spaniards and Portuguese had been the world's most daring explorers and seafarers, nearly all of whom had the single-minded dream of fortune that could be had from the mysterious East.

Christopher Columbus, however, also had a nobler purpose, or at least that was what he had submitted to the Queen and the religious leadership of the court: To bring Christianity to that mysterious but utterly heathen East. Except that, instead of following Marco Polo's *eastern* route over the land, Columbus would dare exploring the *western* route, over the fathomless waves of the open and dreaded ocean which, as most people of the time—including Columbus' own sailors—believed, cascaded as an enormous deluge straight down at the ocean's far end into a cliffhanger of indescribably immense depth.

But Columbus was a brave and informed geographer, firmly believing in the global—or at least conical—shape of the world and, thus, the Eastern land of Hindi and Cathay would be reached if he could successfully navigate his ships westward, straight across the vast ocean. Poor Columbus. He thought he had succeeded in reaching the shores of *East* India, not realizing that he had arrived at an archipelago that later was to be called the *West* Indies.

Worse. For instead of bringing Christianity to the court of the mighty Khans (as Polo in his *Travelogue* had suggested of the mighty Mongol emperor's interest), Columbus and his men turned Christianity into a scourge and, with the help of high-handed slavery and European-brewed diseases, nearly decimated the entire native populations whom he had proclaimed to bring into the Church's fold. In hindsight, it was sad to realize that not only did he not have a sufficiently clear idea of the Christian mission, but he also failed to understand how far *east* is East and how far *west* is West.

How far *east* is East, and how far *west* is West? Here, I am not referring to the actual measurable and quantifiable distance. Rather, I am speaking of the *quality of distance* as well as the *idea of direction*. And since we all know that the earth is spherical, east or west is only a matter of perspective and point of reference, and thus highly relative. In contrast, the idea of north and south is more definite, and can never be confused or reversed. The North Pole is always "up there" and the South Pole is "down there," as we would say. But, east and west? Well, is the United States to the east or west of China? I am not trying to pull a fast one. On the contrary, I am very serious about this. And I would like to pursue this line of thinking by first asking what in the world—literally—is the point of reference when we speak of the East and the West.

Even primitive people had noticed that every day the sun rose from one direction and set in the opposite direction. And the first time the Bible makes a directional reference is with regard to the garden God had planted, in the "*east* of Eden" (and, hence, 'Garden of Eden' is actually a misnomer). The words east and west were of Phoenician origin, and were adopted by the ancient Hebrews as well as the Greeks. Later, these same words had given rise to the now universally adopted words for Asia (east) and Europe (west). In other words, Asia and East are etymologically related and connote the same meaning of the "direction of the sunrise," and Europe and West are likewise related and connote the "direction of the sunset." (In fact, the German word *Abend* means both west and evening.)

This directional distinction was used by the ancient Greeks in referring to the location of lands around them and, hence, all the lands to the east (and northeast) of Greece were called Asia (and the one *smaller* eastern land is called Asia *minor*), while all the lands—a much smaller stretch of land, to be sure—west (and northwest and southwest) of Greece were called Europe. By this Hellenistic view of the world, (the present) India, Turkey, Iran, Iraq, and a host of other countries in that region would be Asian or Eastern, including, of course, (the present) Japan, Korea, China, and the entire Southeast Asian countries. And it would therefore be easy to understand why today we have other more fine-tuned directional references, such as *Near* East, *Middle* East, and *Far* East, all in terms of distance of the regions on the Eurasian continent, all relative to Greece.

This, in reality, means that the vast Eurasian continent stretches from the Atlantic Ocean eastward all the way to the Pacific Ocean, and from the Indian Ocean up northward all the way to the Arctic Ocean, only the very narrow strip of land north and northwest of Italy would be Europe or the West. And we can argue about what portion of Africa and the old Russia (which, as we know, is now not all Russia), or the good-ol' American continents, should belong to Asia or Europe, or some other geographical regions the ancient Greeks had not thought of or had no need of classifying in terms of east or west.

The point of this argument is that, while east and west are a convenient directional reference, from a cultural point of view, such distinction is nearly totally meaningless. And while one culture may seem Eastern to a people, the same may be regarded as quite Western to other people, and the difference is purely a matter of perspective. Is Christianity, in its religious and moral doctrines, not to mention other aspects such as socio-ethical codes and ethnic customs, Eastern or Western? Many readers may be surprised to know that much of it is actually Eastern, although one must acknowledge at the same time that many aspects of its practice are now more Western, due to the Greco-Roman—and later, the European—influences after the New Testament era, and especially after Emperor Constantine. Or, is the idea of democracy Western or Eastern? I can show you passages from ancient Chinese writings where the idea of democratic, just and peaceable government "of the people and for the people" (but not necessarily *by* the people) is pronounced, far more eloquently and convincingly than similar statements in Plato's *Republic* or the *Magna Carta* of thirteenth-century England: Just to cite one such example: the "*Li Yun Da Tong Pian*" by Confucius.

Perhaps it is the writing that distinguishes East and West? After all, we all know that Chinese, Koreans and Japanese write in funny chicken scratches, and going from right to left, while all the Western writings go from left to right. But, of course, we all know that Indian, Arabian, and all Semitic writings go the *Eastern* way—from right to left. But, then, there are certain writings that could go either way, or even any way. If you have ever looked carefully at the ancient Egyptian hieroglyphics, you may have noticed that at times the heads of people (always standing and in a striding pose) face right and at other times face left, but the different "facings" never appear in one particular line of pictographs. This is due to a simple fact that, in Egyptian writing, the direction to which the heads face indicates the direction of writing and reading: if the head faces right, you read from left to right; if the head faces left, you read from right to left. (This manner of writing and reading in alternate direction is referred to as "ox-plow," since the ox will pull the plow in one direction to the end of the plot and turn around and go the reverse direction.)

But why do (the majority of) Eastern writings go from right to left? One explanation is that it was because (the majority of) human beings were (and still are) right-handed (and left-brained). Let me explain. When primitive men began the first "writing" by chiseling on rocks or the surface of cave walls or mud plates, they would of course hold the chisel or some sharp instrument in the left hand and hold the hammer or some blunt and heavy object in the right hand, and would hit away the chisel from right to left.

Unless, of course, you are left-handed. And maybe, just maybe, European ancestors were all left-handed, and right brained.

What, then, distinguishes the Eastern and Western worlds? Culture? Custom? Costume? Or perhaps it is this all-important Color of the skin?

Then one may be tempted to venture an opinion, that perhaps there was more than one Eve and more than one Adam that God had created. That is, God might have created several pairs of Adams and Eves, then put one pair in the sub-Sahara region in Africa, another pair in Europe, in the present Germany or France, and still another—the shortest pair—near Peking in China, and said to these pairs of human couples, in different languages of course, "Be thou to multiply as the sands in the sea and stars in the sky." And the shortest pair who naturally were more humble and obedient, did exactly what the Lord had commanded them, and they multiplied, and multiplied, and kept on multiplying, exponentially. And their descendants—known today as Chinese or *Sinitic* people—now constitute more than one-quarter of the entire human race.

To be sure, there is in the genetic science community a single-Eve theory (led by the pioneering research scientist Dr. Allan Wilson, UC Berkeley), based on the computer generated analysis of DNA, which suggested, several years ago, that a single mother-being lived two to three hundred thousand years ago in Africa south of the Sahara Desert, and that all humans now living or that have ever lived descended from this single woman (and her mate, of course). But, like any theory (even that of Albert Einstein), there are counter-theories, and now this single-Eve theory is under attack.

But, of course, if you believe that the Adam and Eve the Bible speaks of weren't the African type, that they lived in the garden *east* of Eden only about five thousand years ago, then there wouldn't be any problem, since we—the black, brown, white and yellow—are all brothers and sisters, and there isn't—or shouldn't be—such distinction as Easterners or Westerners. That is, until we begin to ask questions such as "where did Abraham and his tribesmen come from?" or "where was this land of Ur?" In reality, Ur (which was in the present Iraq) is closer to Tibet and China than to European West (Italy, Germany, France, and the Great Britain) or America. With this "revelation," we may need to ponder the significance of Abraham being an Asian, that he was the direct ancestor of today's Iraqis. Then we would ask ourselves once again this first question, "Is the East *east* and the West *west*, or what and where is the East and West?"

Certain times of the year, we see in the eastern sky, shortly before the sunrise, a bright star (actually a planet). This is the famous Morning Star (by which name Jesus is also glorified). At certain other times of the year, we see in the western sky, shortly after the sunset, another bright star (planet). This is the Evening Star. But already in the fifth century, B.C.E., Pythagoras had discovered—or surmised—that the eastern Morning Star and the western Evening Star were actually the same celestial body but, due to its position around the sun and relative to the earth's vantage point, may appear to be to the west of the sun (thus rising before the Sun and becoming the Morning Star), or east of the sun (thus setting after the sun and becoming the Evening Star). (The Bible makes several references to this star.) We now know this Evening Star as Venus. But the ancient Greeks called this Venus by two different names: one is Vesper (meaning "west," referring to the Evening Star); the other is Lucifer (meaning the "harbinger of light," referring to the Morning Star). We know, too, that Lucifer is also the name by which Satan is referred to.

This was the same star (or, in this case, planet), but called by different names, and the connotation man gave in naming it was as different as light and darkness. Still, we see it as a beautiful star, and seldom think of the fact that Venus is literally a hell of a planet.

If there is anything we can learn from this, it is that human perception is so subjective and egocentric, that we are often more wrong than right when it comes to understanding the "other" people, the people who don't speak, look, dress, and behave like we do, or people who are bigger or smaller, fairer or darker, dumber of lazier than we are. (We usually don't think, or have a difficult time in accepting, that the "other" people are smarter or more correct than we are. Watch how all those smart people in the U.S. Congress argue endlessly, and you will see what I mean.)

Europeans called Asians heathens and barbarians, and Chinese called Europeans hairy barbarians and *yang-gui* or *yangqui* (sounds like *Yankee*, doesn't it?) that means "the devils from beyond the ocean." (And Japanese regarded European sailors *kusai*—"stinking"). American traveling in Europe often are annoyed by those who don't understand their "English" (with American accents), and would call them '*nitwit.*' (*Nitwit* is actually a corrupt version of a Dutch word to mean "I don't know"). It seems that we all have a tendency to regard other people as inferior. Perhaps that's one quick way we could make us feel good about ourselves, because we are obviously superior than those nitwits since we know what we are talking about, and they don't.

Today, the Western countries—and the United States in particular—are fighting what seems a losing battle against the drug trade, regarding it—and rightfully so—as the very personification of Lucifer. Seldom do we recall the historical fact that, only a century or so ago, the Western alliance—including the United States—forced China to buy their merchandise and the drug opium at gunpoint. With big guns in one hand and the Bible in the other, the Western world forced China to become a country of opium addicts, and drained the wealth—countless *tons* of silver—and sapped the proud spirit of the Chinese people.

Who are the Morning Star and who are the Evening Star? We all are at times Vesper and at other times Lucifer. Asians generally regard Christianity as a Western religion, while the Europeans nearly always regard Buddhism as an Asian religion. As to Greek Orthodox, Judaism, or Muslim, we are not altogether sure which of the East and West categories they should belong. But we are always sure that the one *we* chose is the right one. To paraphrase the lyrics of Ray Evans (in the song "Buttons and Bows" in 1948 movie *The Paleface*),

> "East is east, and West is west
>
> And the wrong one [they] have chose ..."

If a stereotyped image of Muslim is a bearded man wearing a turban, holding the Koran in one hand and a sword in the other, we may see it as an image of the most dreaded in the world: combining a heavenly halo with military might. And, in this, too, there is no difference between East and West. Only the same human beings living east and west of one another, trying all the while to get a little better than the others, driven more by greed and a primitive instinct for survival and less by a sense of brotherly coexistence. And we wonder why God repented that He created man (*cf.* Genesis 6:6)?! Why, indeed. And one may also wonder at the same time whether God looks more like an Eastern or a Western person?

It was right after the end of World War II, and the Christians all over Taiwan were jubilant with the renewed freedom of expressing their faith. For a long time, Christians were closely monitored, scrutinized and even censored by the Japanese government especially in the later years of the war. This sense of Christian revival and jubilation was further bolstered by the return of American missionaries, the instant celebrities, and large masses of people, Christians and non-Christians alike, thronged and followed where these American missionaries went.

Among the early missionary returnees to Taiwan was Dr. James Dickson who was my father's professor back in his theological college days. We had just moved back to Hualien and to a very small church in the rural town of Yu-Li, near my parents' farmland. And my father was truly elated when Rev. Dr. Dickson came especially to visit him. I still remember Dr. Dickson, stout and robust, who, even after all those years, could still speak the Taiwanese dialect, fluently but with a heavy accent.

Then, Sunday came, and many Christians from the tribal villages around Yuli descended and crowded into and overflowed our little church, all desperately trying to catch a glimpse of this first American coming to town. They had seen pictures of Jesus and his disciples, all drawn like clean-cut Caucasian gentlemen, but with beards, of course.

The scene at our church must have resembled the crowd surrounding Jesus when he visited Zaccaeus' hometown. Dr. Dickson, towering over the crowd and yet most gracious and, after the service in which he also spoke briefly, went about the crowd, greeting them and shaking hands.

Afterward, when the crowd had largely scattered, a couple of the tribal men came to my father and confided that they did not shake Dr. Dickson's hand. "But, why? You must!" my father urged. "Oh, No! We just wouldn't dare," they confided. "That huge, hairy hand and arms. Just like a gorilla's. We are scared half to death!" they finally confessed. Then, one of them asked my father, more like murmuring to himself, deep in thought and appeared even troubled:

"I wonder what I would do if Jesus' hands were like Dr. Dickson's?"

2

Chinese, Japanese, and Taiwanese

The early decades of the twentieth century were a period of economic depression in the United States, and the eve of ominous dark clouds in the political landscape in Europe. In the Far East, however, it was an age of glorious political ascent for the island nation of Japan. Shortly before, Japan had won a decisive victory against the invincible army and navy of Imperial Russia and, as war restitution, claimed the southern half of the island of Karafuto (Sakhalin). Emperor Meiji and the English-educated Prime Minister Ito had together brought Japan from the archaic *shogun* feudal society to a modern industrial nation. Within a few decades, Japan was at the forefront of the League of Nations. Everything seemed to be going well for Japan, in spite of the fact that the war with China had stagnated, a war that the Japanese military leadership had overly optimistically predicted initially to be over in a matter of a few months.

Japan was the first-rate and most powerful nation in Asia by the first decades of the twentieth century. The wealth of the nation increased significantly, due in large part to the fact that Japan now had free access to almost inexhaustible natural resources, from coal to iron ore to timbre, from rice to sugar to wheat and corn. For during the last decade of the nineteenth century and the first decade of the twentieth, Japan had claimed vast colonial territories in Korea, Manchuria, and Taiwan, through a series of cunning political-military maneuvers. And while Chiang Kaishek's armies continued their tenacious resistance in the high hinterland of China against pockets of Japanese frontal forces, Japan was quite content to let the war stagnate, since it now also had full access to the fertile coastal provinces as well as world-class commercial ports along the full length of China's shores. It was an age of feeling great to be Japanese, or a part—even as a second-class citizen—of this great Imperial Nation of the "Rising Sun."

This was the era when I was born, on the tiny island of Taiwan (formerly known to the Western world as Formosa), about a hundred miles off the coast of China's mainland, now no longer a Chinese territory but a proud member of the archipelago nation called *Dai Nippon Teikoku*—the Great Imperial Japan. (The name is in parallel with the Great Imperial Britain, also an archipelago nation.)

Beginning in 1895 (the year Taiwan was ceded to Japan), the Japanese had performed miracles on this desolate and forsaken island, transforming literally overnight from a malaria- and pirate- and headhunter infested island with only a few tiny fishing villages and a handful of any sizable municipalities on the west coast, to what the Japanese would soon endearingly call *Takara Zima*, the "Treasure Island." The subtropical island produces two rice crops annually, bountiful and highly prized agricultural produces such as pineapple and sweet potato, and enough sugar to satisfy the entire Japanese sweet tooth. Japanese agricultural scientists made improvement on Taiwan's native rice, and made it fit for the Imperial household's table. (This was the famous *Yoshino No. 2* rice, cultivated near Hualien.) The island was also endowed with rich natural resources of gold, coal, marble, and timbre to supply any government projects.

Two-third mountainous, Taiwan was still a truly viable and mouth-watering piece of real estate. Lying between Japan and the Philippines, it was lush with subtropical forests and plenty of rainfall. When the legendary Portuguese navigator Magellan sailed his ships around the world, his course took him past this island and directly headed toward the Philippines (where Magellan was killed while still on the shore). It was in the later voyages, as the story goes, that the Portuguese sailors were so struck by the beauty of the island that they exclaimed "*Illa formosa!*" ("What a beautiful island!"). Thus the name *Formosa* stuck and, thus known to all the European sailors roaming up and down the coastal seas of China and Japan, the island became the port of call for Portuguese and Dutch navigators for over three centuries until the Japanese occupation. As such—and even during my grandparents' lifetime—Spanish silver coins (the *Reales*) became a part of the currency circulating in Taiwan (as well as in China and Japan), and I still have a few of these *Reales* in my coin collection reclaimed from my maternal grandfather's grave. There are still Dutch architectures in southern Taiwan, including an impressive *Fort of Zelandia*, well preserved, in the present city of Tainan. The locals call this *Fort Zelandia* the "Fort of the *Red Haired People*." I have heard that, once in a great while, a Taiwanese woman would give birth to a pale-skinned, red-haired infant, and the hapless husband would have a fit, accusing the poor wife of unspeakable "*devil*ment" (to Chinese, all the foreigners are *gui* or *qui*, *i.e.* the devils, you know). Perhaps the *genes*—or Genies—of those red-haired sailors may still be lurking deep in some *Formosan* genes even after several centuries.

But, far more than those colonial occupants from the West, or even their own Ming and Qing dynasty court agents, Japan had miraculously transformed this sweet-potato shaped island of some 250 miles by 90 miles to a south-sea paradise, with trans-island railroad and highway systems, an extensive underground sewage system (that, even today, over a hundred years later, could put many mid-size Texas cities

to shame), magnificent modern municipal offices (by securing the services of French and German architects in designing and supervising the
construction of government buildings) and, of course, the modern
public school system, from elementary to middle schools and a number
of technical colleges (similar to U.S.'s A&M colleges), and one university.

It was during the early decades of Japanese occupation of the island
that my parents received all their education. Even my maternal grandfather who, as mentioned earlier, was a Qing dynasty imperial scholar
and a mayor, was so impressed by what the Japanese had done, that he
named his only daughter *Motoko*, meaning "Child of Japan." Later,
ever conscious of the importance of good education (as all Asians
believe, much more so than average Westerners), my parents wanted to
give me nothing less than the best of educational opportunity the new
government on Taiwan offered.

There were two types—or classes—of elementary schools in colonial
Taiwan: One was called *ko-gakko* or 'public' school; the other was
called *sho-gakko* or 'primary' school (later called *jun-jo sho-gakko*,
implying 'liberal arts' primary school). The former was for the
local—that is, the lowly native Taiwanese—kids, while the latter was
reserved exclusively for Japanese children. There was a provision, however, for a selected few—under a *quota* system, just like the "minority"
quota system in today's U.S. college and university admissions mandated by the government—Taiwanese children to be admitted to the
first-grade class every year, two or three to a class. The selection process
was rigorous and stringent, including a review of the educational background of the children's parents, and an official visit to your home to
ensure that Japanese was the primary, if not the only, language spoken
in the home. After all these were deemed satisfactory, the children were
given a day of testing and personal interview, even including a little

'house playing' to see if your manners were adequately refined. (Of all the people from various countries, I know of no other who are more etiquette conscious than the Japanese and Koreans; these two people are siblings historically, culturally, and even ethnically.) And the selected few Taiwanese kids were afforded the privilege of attending the *sho-gakko*, to be taught by Japanese teachers, and to study and play with Japanese children.

In order that I would be properly and thoroughly prepared for sho-gakko, my parents did not allow me to play with the neighborhood Taiwanese kids from the day I was old enough to go outside the house by myself. And I still have fragmented memories of going to the home of my mother's high-school classmate, to learn the proper Japanese manners from her middle-school age daughter, so that my good manners would be as natural as any Japanese, and would pass the close scrutiny of Japanese teachers at the entrance exam. And my passing successfully this exam—the very first in my life—was one of the greatest joys I had brought to my parents. For my mother in particular, that was the first step of her son in fulfilling the dream she once had but was not permitted to realize (*cf.* [THREE], "FROM NUMEROLOGY TO THE CHO FAMILY").

My parents even legally changed our family name Cho to a Japanese name MuneOka. With that, I was a Japanese in every respect. I spoke only Japanese, I was called by a Japanese name Muneoka Hiromasa, I attended a for-Japanese-only school, and I felt ever superior to other local kids. That was, until a few years into World War II, when even a child could sense that something was going awry in what was called *sei-sen*—a 'holy war,' a *jihad*. For even the gallant warriors of "divine wind"—the *kami-kaze* suicidal attack planes) seemed powerless in the face of the advancing American forces in the Pacific. And the once tranquil and abundant life on colonial Taiwan even during the early years of the war was shattered by the ever-increasing air raids by U.S. planes. The government urged the populace to evacuate to rural villages where the danger and destruction of air raids would be minimal. And my parents sent us children and my grandmother to a tiny rural community—not even a village, just a handful of farm houses a couple of hundred yards from each other—several miles further up the hillsides from the train station of the town of *Wudan* (or *Botan-Ko* during the Japanese days).

The life of evacuation, living in a remote farming village, also had turned out to be one of the most precious of my childhood memories. It was there that I came to a fuller understanding of who I was, through the intimate reacquaintance with the old lady living in our house—my maternal grandmother. For all the years prior to the evacuation, I had seldom—in fact, I could never recall ever having—talked to her, since she did not know any Japanese, and I could not speak a word of Taiwanese dialect. During the months of living in that tiny farm village, in a rented bedroom, I learned to speak my first few Taiwanese words and soon well enough to converse with my grandmother for the first time. I also managed to foster a close friendship with and nearly every day played with one particular, utterly illiterate and ignorant (so I thought) boy from a poor farmer's house a couple of hundred yards further up the hillside. He taught me to steal and eat cucumbers, unwashed and uncooked, and showed me how to catch fish in the small streams. Eventually I learned to catch tiny shrimp and crabs with my bare hands, and right away toss these little creatures right into my mouth. It was a time when nearly everyone was hungry, particularly the young boys who were growing up fast.

The end of the war, and Taiwan was back to the bosom of her motherland. No longer were we second-class citizens, and all the people in Taiwan were truly jubilant. That jubilation was short lived. For we laid our eyes on the first Chinese troops, the conquering heroes who defeated the mighty Japanese armies and who now had come to reclaim the poor and long-oppressed people of Taiwan.

And what a sight! What was sent to Taiwan were sorry ragtag bands of peasants, with straw shoes and ill-fitted uniforms. Most of these 'soldiers' were illiterate, and utterly primitive, carrying on their backs pots and pans instead of military arms, and many of them had never seen any of the modern facilities before arriving in Taiwan. Soon after the arrival of a platoon in our small town, a story was circulated that a soldier went back to a store to return the faucet he had just bought, complaining that it was defective, and wanted his money back. The store manager asked why he knew the faucet was defective. The peasant solder replied: "I took it to my barrack and *stuck it on the wall and turned the handle*, but no water came out!"

The Chinese from the mainland, now seeing themselves as the deliverers of Taiwan but acting more like conquerors and masters of an occupied land, further helped to intensify the disappointment and disdain of the islanders. The tension mounted at every turn of events and, finally, it exploded in the now infamous "Two-Two-Eight Incident" (so called because the 'uprising' began on February 28). Bands of militant Taiwanese—many the ex-soldiers of the Japanese army—felt that they, and not the sorry vagabonds from China's hinterland, should manage the affairs of the people of the Island, and took actions. I still remember the day when suddenly the students were dismissed and were told to return home quickly and orderly. When a few of us were walking past the public sports field on top of a hill, we were amazed to see a band of men in Japanese army uniforms, tending to a few machine guns and rifles, not realizing that the situation was serious, that there would be terrible consequences.

Indeed, the Chinese government quickly responded and retaliated most harshly, sending armies to summarily round up who ever they regarded as the instigators and cohorts of the 'uprising.' One night the government agents and soldiers were dispatched to countless homes of the prominent figures on the Island. Many of them, intellectuals, medical doctors and lawyers, were arrested. Among them were my father's high school classmate, a medical doctor, and his three sons. Their hands were bound with wires, and led away. Later they were found dead, drowned in the lake, with the wires still on their wrists. All this atrocities were committed without any trial.

It took more than two generations for the people of Taiwan to turn the disdainful regards for the "mainlanders"—mostly army personnel in Chiang's army—to something resembling a feeling for fellow countrymen, although, even today, the two distant kin folks do not always see eye to eye when it comes to political matters. Taiwanese regard themselves not wholly like the mainland-Chinese, but neither would they acknowledge that they are Japanese. For better or worse, the Japanese during their fifty-year occupation of Taiwan and through a relentless educational process, surely had done a superb and thorough job in altering the character of the people of Treasure Island, molding it into something of a mixture of Japanese and Chinese ethnic temperaments.

An "ethnic what?" Yes, ethnic *temperament*. And there is a great deal of disparity between the temperament and demeanor of the Chinese and Japanese people as two distinct ethnic and cultural peoples. To be sure, the difference is perhaps greater than, say, between Americans and Europeans. To explain the differences, even superficially, will require a rather lengthy and complex discourse. In fact, the differences are in minute details of fine degree, such that a verbal explanation of them is all but impossible. Instead, I would like to conclude this article with a story—an ethnic joke, if you would—just to ask the readers to please kindly refrain from ever saying that Chinese, Japanese, Koreans, and Taiwanese are all alike.

One day a little Chinese man entered a Jewish delicatessen for a corn-beef sandwich lunch, and sat down next to the table where a bully of a Jewish customer happened to be sitting. Taking a quick scrutinizing glare, the Jewish hunk walked over to this Chinaman and, without rhyme or reason, slapped him hard, then walked back to his table. Startled and humiliated, the Chinese demanded to know why.

"It's a revenge for my cousin who died at Pearl Harbor," growled the Jewish hunk.

"But, sir," the little man protested,

"I didn't have anything to do with Pearl Harbor or the War.

And, look, Sir, I am a Chinese, not Japanese."

"Chinese, Japanese, HA!" spit the hunk; "They're all the same."

The little man sat down and looked at his sandwich, pitifully. For awhile. Then he stood up, all five feet and one inch tall. Walking over to Mr. Hunk and, with all his might, he swung his small fist against the big target of a face.

"Hey, Yellow! What in hell …" the big face bellowed.

"Ah, Sir. I am avenging for my honorable great, great, great uncle who died when Titanic sank," the little man replied.

"Ti-TAH-nic!?" exploded the big fellow.

"Don't you know. STUPID, that Titanic was sunk by an iceberg?"

"Ah, soh sorry," apologized the Chinese, grinning toothily.

"But, I thought, Goldberg, Rosenberg, Iceberg, they're all the same!"

3

From Numerology to the Cho Family

This article is the third in this "The East is East, and the West is West" series, and my sixth article to appear in the Flower Mound, TX weekly paper, *Pipeline*. Both of these numbers, three and six, possess special significance, and in fact were regarded as particularly auspicious numbers. The root of the idea of attaching certain significance to numbers goes back to the dawn of human culture and, in all ancient civilizations, the knowledge of number and the ability to manipulate numbers were highly prized. In fact, this 'wisdom of numbers' was regarded in early societies as the privileged domain of people of the upper castes who were empowered to rule the lives of the commoners. They were the castes of the rulers and the priests.

Specifically, the number THREE was regarded as signifying things celestial or spiritual, as opposed to the number TWO which was more mundane and common. The reason for such bestowal of connotation is that "three points define the size of an arc or a circle" and, by extension, represent the 'heavenly dome,' while "two points delineate a line" or flat surface and, by extension, represents the earthly plain, a flat earth.

The number SIX is, of course, the product of multiplying two and three, and expresses a 'harmonious relationship' between or conjoining of heaven and earth, or, between god and man. From the early dawn of human civilization such as in the Sumerian culture and mythology, the number six was regarded as the most beautiful number and even regarded as signifying the creative wisdom of god. It was this sort of reasoning and in the heritage of the cultural lineage from the Sumerians to the early Greeks and other ancient societies in the Fertile Crescent all the way to Central Asia, India, and the Far East, that the "number game" was not only propagated but was taken very seriously. In fact, the ancient Greeks—the intellectuals of the early *old world* cultures—regarded the number six as the "most perfect of all *perfect numbers.*"

In the number game—the Greeks called it *geometria* (geometry) from which the corrupt version *gematria* came—the perfect number is one that is the sum of all its factorials. Six has three factorials (the numbers which can evenly divide the original number): one, two, and three. One + two + three equals six, making it a perfect number. Twenty-eight is also a perfect number: the sum of its factorials [one + two + four + seven + fourteen] will indeed yield twenty-eight. But the number six has one particular attribute that no other perfect numbers possess: the product (*i.e.*, multiplication) of its factorials also equals the number, as $[1 \times 2 \times 3] = [1 + 2 + 3] = 6$.

The ancients had also realized that the number six is "written" in nature all around them. For example, there are six wanderers (the *planets*) in the nightly sky, flowers have six petals, honeycombs are hexagonal, and even insects have six legs. (And, had they had microscopes, they would have noticed, too, that snowflakes are forever hexagonal even in their endlessly different designs.) Hence the Greeks as well as many ancient mystics saw in this the perfect beauty of the wisdom of creative design. It is not difficult therefore to understand why the ancient wise men had fathomed the idea (as in the Sumerian creation story) that god had created this beautiful world in six days. The important point here is not so much the number itself (*six* days) but, rather, the significance of perfect beauty that this number connotes ("God saw that it was *good*").

This branch of inquiry is called numerology. To be sure, it is a pseudo science where numbers were bestowed with meanings, and was called *geometria* by ancient Greeks and *gematria* by the Hebrews. Indeed, *gematria* was regarded as a serious subject matter not only by the ancient Greeks, Egyptian and Semitic people, and even Chinese, but had remained so and highly regarded particularly in the medieval monastic institutions in Europe until the relatively recent past.

This pseudo science is still practiced by many modern Chinese. For example, when a child is born, the numbers from the month, the day, and the hour of the infant's birth were all taken into formulating a number series, and diagnosed, usually by fortune-tellers or by consulting the divination books. These numbers relating to the infant's birth are regarded as the celestial signs that would foretell the fortune of the child's life. Chinese parents would also devote considerable care in selecting the name of the child, carefully counting the number of strokes in the child's written name. For they believe that there are good numbers and bad numbers, strong and weak numbers. Sometimes the parents would purposely give a child an awful name, if his birth numbers (month, day, hour of birth) connote a bad omen. And the parents would want to give their child a awful name, in the hope that the devil would regard someone with such a terrible name not worth their bother, and would go elsewhere to play their evil mischief.

You see, numbers are serious matters and are believed to represent a person's character. And we all have heard about the "number of the beast" mentioned in the Bible (Revelation Chapter 13): "six hundred and sixty six." (This is quite different from the "holy and perfect" number six, and I will offer an explanation in another article of this "number of the Beast.") For now, I simply could not resist taking advantage of the concurrence of two auspicious numbers, three and six, and making this an occasion for personal note. After all, my parents named me "Benevolent Auspiciousness": that is the literal meaning of my Chinese given name, JIN-SIONG (or REN-XIANG in Mandarin pronunciation). This article, therefore, is a personal pilgrimage back to my life's past, by sharing with readers some notable notes from the pages of the history of my immediate family.

◆   ◆   ◆

My paternal grandfather was a simple farmer who had never attended a day of school and therefore was illiterate all his life. His father died young, still in his thirties, from wounds he suffered while fending off a band of aborigines bandits who descended on his house one night to rob and set fire to the house. (The aborigines were tribal people who had come from South China-Sea islands centuries before and had settled on Taiwan long before the Chinese began to populate the small island.)

My grandparents were the first Cho to venture out of the Cho ancestral village in northern Taiwan. (There, until recently, was a Cho village near modern city of Taoyuan, near the Chiang Kaishek International Airport. In the old days, everyone in the village—from the mayor to the beggars—had the surname Cho). My grandmother was converted to Christianity before being married to my grandfather, and subsequently had led her husband to the faith. This had aroused spurn from the village kinfolks, and my grandparents chose to leave the comfort of the home village, rather than disavowing their faith. And they moved to the far eastern mountainous region of Taiwan, south of modern city of Hualien, across the river and valley from the present township of Fonglin. The area was mostly uncultivated, with only a handful of daring—or desperately poor—farmers attempting to culti-vate a little plot of land they could call their own.

These were the wild frontier days as recent as the late nineteenth century, and all Chinese settlements were on the western side of the Island. These early settlers avoided the mountainous areas especially on the east coast, as these areas were the terrains controlled by the "moun-tain tribes" who were still headhunters. A few years after the Japanese first occupied Taiwan (ceded to Japan in 1895 as a part of restitution for the Sino-Japanese war which the *Qing* dynasty lost), a band of tribal warriors descended on a Japanese elementary school on the day of field exercise, and massacred all the Japanese and Taiwanese attending the festivity, adults, children and all, including a few high-ranking Japa-nese officials sent there to observe the festivity. In retaliation, the Japa-nese government sent in armies and even planes to drop incineration bombs on the tribal villages.

My grandparents raised six sons and two daughters; the youngest child, a daughter, had to be given away for adoption because my grandmother died in giving birth. Before her life was cut short, she had managed to lead her entire family to the Christian faith. In fact my grandparents were among the very first fruits of the missionary works of Dr. McKay, the first missionary to Taiwan, who took a local servant maid as his wife. It was through Dr. McKay's hands that my grandpar-ents received baptism. I still own a copy of the original photo of my grandparents with their seven children and my father in the lap of his mother, taken by Dr. McKay more than a century ago.

These were awfully difficult days even for daily survival, not unlike the frontier days of the wild west of America. You had to go a few hun-dred yards to carry drinking water, and you could never be sure you were going to make it back safely every time you went out, since ambush by the aborigines was a not-so-infrequent occurrence. My father who was the youngest of the six boys often told us the story that, on one of his regular days of watching the family herd of water buffaloes, he somehow sensed uneasiness, and ran straight home, leaving the herd behind. For this, my father was scolded for cowardliness by his eldest brother, and was forced to go back to the cattle site with him. No sooner did they reach the spot than rifle shots rang out from behind the nearby bushes. Later, my uncles found their neighbor's farmhouse ransacked, cattle gone, and their bodies lying around, literally without their heads. This was one of the two reasons my father had later decided to become a minister, in gratitude and servitude to the Lord who had spared his life.

But I am a bit ahead of myself. I need to go back to pick up a few details about my grandparents, both paternal and maternal.

Though illiterate all his life, this simple farmer, now without the help of his wife, decided to raise all his seven children (the eighth child was given away for adoption). Though weighed down with the burden of subsistence, he endeavored to give his children schooling—any amount of schooling. For this was what his wife had always wished.

These were the early days of Japanese occupation and, in order to bring the natives to their fold, the Japanese government not only provided free education but also actually paid money to parents to encourage sending their children to school. Even that posed difficulty for poor farmers, since every pair of able hands was needed, and each one in the family, no matter how young, had assigned chores. After going to school for two years, my father was called back home, and was assigned the duty of watching the family herd of water buffaloes. For nine years he watched the herd. Finally, at the insistence of his third brother's wife who was my father's surrogate mother, he was allowed to go back to school, as a third grader, already a mid-teenager. Of the six boys, two had managed to finish middle school, and my father was the only one to go further, to graduate from theological college. Today, the Cho family, out of this simple farmer's sons and their sons and grandsons, can list more than thirty ministers. You see, my grandfather's last words were "Love one another, treat one another justly, and spread the Gospel."

My maternal grandparents were of quite a different story. My maternal grandfather was orphaned when he was very young, and was adopted by a kind but poor couple who had him watch the family cattle, as they too could not afford to send him to school. In those days there was no public school in Taiwan; there were only private tutoring "chambers" requiring tuition payment. But this lad, my "future" grandfather, would often waste away his day hours standing outside the window of a private school house, looking inside and listening, instead of minding his cattle-watching chore. After awhile, the teacher became curious, and subsequently convinced his adopted parents to let him attend school. The parents could not afford the tuition, but together they came to an agreement that the lad would do the teacher's house chores in exchange for education. The lad advanced quickly and, years later, he took and passed the government's "imperial exam" and was assigned a government post. He became a mayor of his home district, and retired from that position when he was too old to manage the town's administrative duty. During his lifetime he also erected a school and became the only teacher there, encouraging the town's people and especially the poor farmers to send their children for education, all free of charge.

It was during his tenure as the mayor of Bali (across the river from Tamsui and Taipei) that Taiwan was ceded to Japan. And these were the days where no civil laws governed the land, where thieves and bandits roamed rampant. Once, my grandfather was arrested by the Japanese police under the suspicion of harboring a fugitive, a local 'Robin

Hood,' and was imprisoned. After a few days, the guards came and took him out and shaved his hair, and he thought his end had surely come. (It was the custom to cut the hair of the criminal on the day of execution, so that the hair would not get in the way of making a clean chopping.) But, inexplicably, my grandfather and his accomplice, who was the bandit's wife, were let go. Shortly before my grandfather died at age 81 and already blind, my mother brought her month-old infant son to visit her father. I was told that he had touched me, beamed, felt difficult to conceal the joy that his only daughter now had given him a grandson. When I was in high school and again in university, I visited Bali, my grandparents' mayoral estate, and the plot of land where the school he had built once stood. For his dedication and contribution as a scholar, educator, and a legendary just and merciful mayor (for example, he would pay off the taxes of many who could not afford to bear the financial burden), he was honored as one of the "Ten Gentlemen of Taiwan" and was sent on an official visit to Tokyo, and the privilege of an audience with Emperor Meiji.

His first wife died quite early, and he remarried when he was thirty-six years old, already a mayor, by taking as his wife a local illiterate maiden eighteen years his junior. There is a story that I simply must share with you about how this imperial scholar-mayor had decided on that illiterate maiden to be his wife. The following story was told and retold to us the siblings while we were all very young, by the mayor's wife—our grandmother.

One evening this mayor was sitting at the doorway of his mayoral mansion (I still remember the U-shaped residence compound, with a large inner courtyard, surrounded by a thick-walled fence about ten feet high, with portholes—gun holes—on the walls to fight and ward off bandits) when a band of tea-picking maidens passed by the mayoral residence after a day of labor on the hills. The mayor noticed one particular girl or, more specifically, he noticed the maiden's very small feet. You see, in those days, the beauty of a Chinese lady was measured—literally—by the size of her feet; the smaller and daintier the more beautiful. For a pair of dainty little feet would indicate that the maiden was of high birth and wealthy household, while big feet belonged to girls who ran around doing all the house and farm chores. (The American girls' oversized feet are for quite another function that I should not elaborate here.) For it was the custom of the day that parents would begin binding the feet of their daughters while they were yet toddlers. My grandmother was born into a relatively wealthy merchant family, and her feet were bound when she was very, very young. When she was about six years old, misfortune befell her family, and her parents lost their fortunes, and she had to be sold, literally, to another family, as a maid, as a partial payment for the parents' debt.

This was a common custom in those days of old China, and I can still recall my grandmother recounting the stories of her harsh life as a maid: rising before the cock crowed to start the fire in an earthen stove, to cook breakfast for the master's family; getting severely punished when she was found nodding and dozing off in front of the warm fire in the wee hours of the cold morning, and eating the leftovers only after everyone in the family had finished the meal. Later, in her teens, she was sent to the hills to pick tealeaves to supplement the family income. In spite of her harsh life, she loved singing, and I have been told many times that her "singing voice would echo in the tea-farming valleys."

One day, these tea-picking girls were having their lunch under a large linden tree when a passerby stopped and asked for a drink of water from the girls. As a gesture of thanks, this stranger offered to read their palms—fortune telling, you see. And reading the palm of this poor maid—this, my future grandmother—he said one day she would become a **shian-shi"-nyu** (*note*: the superscript *"* indicates that *shi* is to be pronounced with a nasal sound), that is, "Mrs. Official." My grandmother would beam whenever she retold the story: "I simply laughed and laughed. How could this ever be possible! I was a poor maid, never had a day's schooling!"

As I was saying, this lonely imperial scholar-mayor so happened to notice this poor tea-picking maiden's feet. It was—and still is—rude and impolite to gaze at another person's face, but looking at another person's feet wasn't discourteous. But I would suspect that Mayor Wang must also have taken at least a quick glance at the maiden's face, and noticed that it wasn't too bad either. Looking at and being attracted by a pair of dainty little feet is one thing, but sooner or later you would have to look up and notice the face, and you certainly wouldn't want to find any surprise there. And, so, being the mayor, he had the resources to dispatch his staff to inquire about the availability of the rest of the body above the ankles of that pair of dainty feet. That was exactly how they got married.

My mother was their second child (the first child, also a daughter, died when she was about eight years of age). Like her father, my mother was a lover of books, and did extremely well in school. Her excellent schoolwork, fine poetry writing, and eloquent oratory skills were such that she was nominated for, and received the full scholarship, including living stipends, from the Taiwan government for university education in Japan.

This didn't happen, however. You see, her father was nearly seventy years old then, and he simply couldn't wait any longer for his only daughter to get married, settled, and bear him a grandchild or two. Besides, in those days, most girls didn't even get to finish elementary school education, and his daughter was graduating from high school—far too much education already for a girl. And he would hear none of this foolishness about his daughter going far away to a university in Japan, leaving the old dad behind, forever wondering when he might be able to hear the pitter-patter of his grandchild's feet in his house.

This father-daughter confrontation over the "to go or not to go" issue finally came to an abrupt end when, one evening over the supper table, the yet teenage daughter again broached the subject. And she was so insistent, even adamant, in pursuing her dream overseas. Thereupon the old mayor completely lost his imperial scholar's cool and, in a fit of rage, he grabbed the family cat near his lap and flung it against the wall, killing the poor critter instantly. It was a cruel show of his opinion, but the message was abundantly clear; my mother knew that she might be next. So, she obligingly behaved like a good Chinese daughter, and consented to marry a certain young man who had gotten into the mayor's favor: my future father.

This young man was just graduating from high school and preparing to enter a theological college. He frequently visited his elder brother who happened to be the minister of the small church in the mayor's town. The mayor liked the younger brother of the minister, particularly his upright and extremely courteous demeanor, a strong silent type who treated elders with great respect. This young man was four years older than the mayor's daughter, old enough and with a good potential to "subjugate" his free-willed daughter.

Often as a child listening to my mother recounting the stories of how her father had "made" her marry my father, I somehow felt a measure of debt to that poor cat, for my chance at this life. Incidentally, this is my reason for not believing in reincarnation. I would rather NOT face that cat, in this life or the next.

Why did this mayor choose this young man who was then just entering a theological college, to be the life companion of his only daughter who already was a schoolteacher? This imperial and Confucian scholar had been converted to the Christian faith only recently, through a rather miraculous experience of faith during a serious illness. And, I am sure, he could not think of anyone more trust-worthy to leave his only daughter with than a man who was to become a servant of his newfound God. And he was so right in his choice. Rev. Henry Cho served in the ministry for over fifty years, during which he had established three churches, all from the ground-zero level up, never wanting to seek ministerial positions with nice stipends. His motto for ministry was a simple one: "God does not accept the second best of our efforts" (*cf.* James 4:17). But, more characteristically, he also had a rather peculiar philosophy for his own ministry: "Minister to the people in poor churches, for there you will see the will of God more clearly."

Rev. Henry Cho and Mrs. Tsunhua Wang Cho had raised six children: four daughters and two sons. There are four ministers in the family today: two sons-in-law, one son, and one grandson. Rev. Cho died in March 1991, at age 91, in Dallas, Texas; Mrs. Cho passed away in January 2003, three months shy of her 99th birthday, in Denton, Texas, and was laid to rest next to her husband of nearly seventy years of their earthly life together.

4

Happy Lunar New Year

About this time last year I had an article in *Pipeline* about new years and the Chinese new year in particular. I mentioned a few things about calendars that the ancient Eastern and Western cultures had in common. On Saturday, February First, my wife and I were invited to a Chinese new year's party in Denton, sponsored by the Chinese Student Organization of the University of North Texas and Texas Woman's University. And since I happened to be the only Chinese professor from these two universities attending the festivity, I was asked to speak briefly, to welcome the guests, many of whom were American or, at least non-Asian. Frankly, I was not at all prepared to give any speech, let alone one with any noteworthy thoughts to share. As I sat at the table trying to think of something halfway intelligent or amusing to say, I glanced at the front wall of the large hall and saw a huge red-letter banner with the following letters:

[HAPPY LUNAR NEW YEAR]

Like a drowning man desperately trying to grab a few straws to stay afloat, I gazed at this sign and tried to come up with some organized thoughts. I looked at the word LUNAR, and a few ideas began to come together. And, so, when I was called to the podium, I was ready. Here, I would like to recall and share my remarks that night while still fresh in my mind, and to add a few more pieces of information in order to make this article a much more organized narrative than my *impromptu* talk that night.

◆   ◆   ◆

From time immemorial, mankind has been fascinated by waxing and waning of the Moon's shining phase. With its definite cycle of the periods of changing phases, the Moon was regarded by all early men to be nature's timepiece. All ancient civilizations, from the Sumerians who are considered as the earliest human intellectuals, to the Babylonians and the Chinese, began to fathom their own calendars all to align with the cycle of the Moon's changing phases. Such LUNAR calendars which, even today, are observed by the Chinese and Koreans (but less so by the Japanese) as well as all the people of the Muslim faith, are based on the cycle of alternating twenty-nine and thirty day months. This is a happy compromise between the lunar months that are about 29.5-days long. Six 29-day months and six 30-day months will make one *Lunar* year about 354 days long. This is about eleven days shorter than the *Solar* year. The solar year consists of 365+ (about one-fourth) days long and, as we all know, is much more accurate than the lunar year in terms of annual cycle of seasonal changes. The earliest civilization that fully adopted the solar calendar was the Egyptian, the children of River Nile, whose life was regulated by the cycle of flooding that occurred as regularly as clockwork.

We know, too, that the solar year calendar makes adjustment once every four years, by inserting a day at the end of February, in order to make up for the shortage in the 365-day yearly cycle. This is the "leap" year, because in that year the progress of monthly days will "leap" over sequentially progressing weekdays of the same month-day a year before or a year after. For example, if March the first this year falls on Monday, we can be sure that March the first next year will fall on Tuesday.

But if next year is a "leap" year, its March the first will skip over a weekday and will fall on Wednesday.

We Americans celebrate this leap year, once every four years, by the frenzied—and increasingly commercial and comical—presidential election hooplas. But, to be sure, this is not entirely correct. For example, the Centennial year was supposed to be a leap year, but the month of February had twenty-eight days, instead of 29. Explanation please: the centennial year that is divisible by 400 is NOT to be a leap year. This omission of a leap year once every four centuries is for the purpose of making another fine-tuning in adjusting and correcting the slight "getting ahead" in the precise sun-earth rotation relationship. You see, the ratio between the period of rotation of the earth on itself (one day), and the period of its rotation around the sun (one year) is in an irrational—that is, a never-ending—proportion.

Not only the periods of rotation of the earth and the sun are in such a slipshod relation, but also the moon's period of rotation about the earth is slipshod, and this forces the people who adopt the lunar calendar to make various adjustments; we in the West have the leap year and the leap day (February 29), while the Asians have "leap month," adding a whole month every three years on the average. This is their "leap" month (no Asians would call *leap* month, but I am sure you wise readers would immediately understand the connotation). If you happened to be born in the leap day (in the West) or the leap month (in Asia), you will either have to forego three birthday celebrations, or have two birthdays in one year. I suppose there are people who happened to be born in a leap year and thus save the trouble (or miss the occasion) of the birthday festivity. There was such a person, a composer by the name of Gioachino Rossini. He was rather lazy as composer goes, loved to eat (and thus extremely fat), and managed to celebrate his birthday only nineteen times during his seventy-six year life.

Besides the fact that the very concept of the length of a month was based on the cycle of the Moon's changing phases, the origin of the length of a week can also be traced back to this most wonderful of all nature's phenomena. It seems that the Babylonians already had a lunar month divided into four equal periods, coinciding with one of the four waxing-waning phases of the Moon—approximately seven and a half day long. Rounding it to seven, the ancient astrologers also designated each of the seven star-gods to rule each of the seven days of the moon-phase. Hence, we still have SUN(day), MO(O)N-day, and so forth, to SATUR(N)-day. Our English weekday names are not as immediately revealing on this star-god-to-weekday relationship as other languages such as French or Spanish. In French, for example, Tuesday is called MARdi (for Mars day), Wednesday is called MERCREdi (for Mercury day), Thursday is JEUdi (for Jupiter day), and Friday is VENDREdi (for Venus day). However, the English word "week" had its origin in an old Germanic word that meant "change" (*wechseln* in the modern German), clearly in reference to the "changing phases of the Moon."

We know or have heard about the effect of the Moon on human life. The Moon was a particularly important factor in the life of all ancient man, East or West. Today, while the Moon no longer mystifies us (modern man), scientists would tell us that, without the Moon, its gravitational pulls which cause the ocean tides, life might not have been possible on this earth. But even in this scientific age, the fairy tales about the Moon linger on in every culture, likening it to a beautiful and mysterious maiden, or to the hours that cause the vampires and werewolves to lurk among human victims.

Even for those who do not believe in such medieval horror tales, the Moon conjures up a romantic sentiment. Under the pale Moon light, lovers are "moon-struck," and would whisper the wooing phrases like "though far apart, I can see your smiling face in the moon over me."

They certainly are innocent and gullible sorts. I, for one, would utterly resent this line of flattery and, in fact, would take it as an insult. Anyone who had really looked at the Moon could tell that its face is full of pockmarks. And I don't like to be called a "pockmarked moon face." But I guess I am not the romantic sort. I am a Moon-Gazer of quite a different persuasion. Let me explain.

I teach music at the University of North Texas. Actually, I don't teach the technical aspect of music making. Instead, I teach what is called "music theory"—a misnomer, to be sure, but the term has been in existence for over a thousand years. Music theorists, just in case you don't have a clear idea about this revered (?) profession, are a band of people who, talent-wise, have been slightly short-changed. We are not as artistically gifted to be performers, nor are we sufficiently inspired to be composers, and neither are we the strong, dictatorial type to be conductors. Still, we love music just the same and, therefore, we give ourselves to the task of theorizing or, in other words, simply talking, discoursing and forever arguing *about* anything remotely related to music.

You see, in the history of human civilization, we the music theorists belong to a profession that was one of the most revered (?) of all the learned societies in all ancient cultures, East and West, from Babylonian to Egyptian to Greek to Chinese, and in the ancient Hebrew society, this group of people was referred to as the Levites, the tribe to which Moses and Aaron belonged.

Levites and the likes in all ancient cultures were the stargazers, or *Lunarians*. They were the philosophers, the "lovers of wisdom" and the brotherhood of the Pythagoreans. Their appointed tasks in the society were to observe the position of the "fixed" stars and the movement of the wandering stars (the planets), and to record the changes in season. They made inquiry of the relationship of all things visible and invisible, and they possessed the wisdom of writing and counting. From their observation of the natural universe, they began to fathom the laws of causal effects between things, and between numbers and matters. This also led them to discover the relationship between numerical ratio and music intervals and, instead of being content with the beauty of musical sounds, they "theorized" themselves into believing that music affects human mind, human soul, human society, and even the cosmic spirit. They didn't stop there; since they discovered that numerical ratios were intimately related to musical intervals, the numbers would also have causal effect on not only the state of man but also his life's fortune and his entire personality.

O the joy and wonder of theoretical philosophizing. If numerical ratios are intimately related to musical sounds, then everything that can be represented by number can be an element of sound, so they theorized, and then boldly claimed it to be the truth. This was called the *doctrine of ethos* that would posit a stance, a philosophical perspective that the whole creation visible and invisible can be represented by numbers and ratios, and the entire cosmos is filled with the glorious harmony of God's creation. Such a belief is inferred in the Bible, for example, when it states that "the morning stars sing together" (Book of Job).

In the ancient worlds, East and West, kings and rulers sought the advice of the lunarians on matters of rituals of the season (such as the time of planting and the time of harvesting) and even on matters of—and the prognostication of—the fortunes of war. In other words, the lunarians were at the same time mathematicians, theologians, astrologers, and geometricians, all wrapped into one. (Astrologers were plain astronomers but with a healthy dose of mysticism.) As such, they were the go-betweens, the oraclers and communicators between human rulers and kings and the heavenly rulers and kings—the gods.

In fact, until the relatively recent past (as late as the Renaissance period), music theory was one of the four "upper-division" subjects which all who claimed to be properly educated were required to take: these four subjects, collectively called the *Quadrivium* (the "four-branched road") were arithmetic, astrology, geometry, and music theory which was then called "harmony" (the word which in fact referred to the study of ratio). And, of course, the lunarians, or the people who were equipped with the knowledge of these four subjects, were revered as "philosophers"—the lovers of wisdom. There is good reason why the lunarians were believed to be the communicator and the interpreter between god and man. First, if things can be represented by numbers and if sounds are but numerical ratios "made audible" (as Pythagoras is said to have explained), then the language of god must be numbers and not human words. God created the universe with the wisdom of number, and the only humans able to understand that wisdom were the lunarians.

Hence, the same line of theorizing continues, humans cannot talk to god using human language. Instead, humans must use numbers to communicate with god. But how can you speak numbers? For you cannot hear the numbers. Ah, but you can hear the music which is a representation of numbers. So, soon the lunarians and the ancient Hebrew Levites also oversaw and administered the ritual music, to make sure that the music was acceptable to god. In other words, besides all these elevated positions in the ancient society, lunarians were also the "choir directors." They determined which song to sing, how to sing it, what is the correct tempo and the proper key, all according to the seasonal requisites. If the music was not correctly performed, then the numbers "in" the music would not be correct. Then the music would not be acceptable to god, since the music would not be effective in carrying the people's propitiation to god.

There were times, however, when god didn't seem to answer the people's prayer no matter how correct the music was, and the lunarian-music priests would rant, blaming it all on the singers and players (just like the choir directors today still do). Sometimes things got out of hand, the situation became intolerable, and singers and players would revolt against the unfair and unfounded reproaches of the lunarian priests and, instead of referring to them as *lunarians*, they would call them the ranting and haranguing *lunatics*. Because they just lost it, the temper and behavior of these self-claimed moon-dwellers were negatively affected by the changing phases of the Moon.

The Moon has shone over the earth for billions of years, its period of rotation changed over these eons of ages, and its phase toward the earth also. Yet its mystique remains, and its effect also the same whether in ancient times or today, on the Easterners or on the Westerners. And, so, whether or not you observe the Lunar New Year, may your life be as bright and full as the Moon on the night of Mid-Autumn Festival.

5

Heavenly Halo and Earthly Crown

I could still remember vividly, even after so many years, the first time I had US money to call my very own, bills and coins and all. It was on my very first flight to the United States, and the plane made a stop at Honolulu Airport where the passengers went through US customs. There I exchanged my precious few Taiwanese dollars for US currencies, and I even bought my very first "MADE IN USA" item—a shaving razor that, to this day, is still in my possession, although I had stopped using it many years ago. That was when I had the opportunity to carefully scrutinize US money, and saw the inscription [**IN GOD WE TRUST**], and I thought "Wow, no wonder America is so great!"

That was many decades ago, in my more impressionable days. But even during my first year in the United States, I began to see that "In God We Trust" was not a creed that people put into practice in their daily lives and that, in America, the name of God was actually—and more often than not—taken in vain. Here in America, even if the Constitution proclaims that all men are equal in God's sight, people certainly are far from being equal in the sight of their fellow men.

The first time I was made keenly aware of this was on my Trailways bus trip from Seattle, WA to Greenville, SC, about two months after I arrived in the United States. I left Seattle late one evening, for a weary two-day and three-night bus trip. Somewhere halfway on the journey—I wasn't too familiar with US geography then—the bus again made the now familiar half-hour stop, to allow the weary travelers to get off the bus to stretch their benumbed and sore bodies, visit the restaurants and use the toilets. I headed toward the rest room, but halted at the doorway. There were *the* signs:

For Whites Only

---

on one side, and

For Coloreds Only

---

on the other.

I hesitated; should I classify myself a white or a color? Looking down at my arms, I decided that I should opt for a "safer" door, the **[COLOREDS]**, not wanting to be thrown out for being in the wrong place and the wrong skin color.

I went in and stood at the watering hole, and heard another man coming. He came and stood right next to me, not even half a foot away. I looked his way, and I looked *up*. He was truly huge—very tall and very black, and he stared down at me without a word. Not that I had expected him to say anything, but his probably innocent or, more likely, curious look (of "what is this *Chinaman* doing here" sort of look) was to me more like a scrutinizing glare of an executioner before lowering his ax. My heart pounded fast. For a moment I truly feared that HE was going to throw me out, because I was not the correct color tint.

After arriving at the campus, I was told that each student ought to have his own bed linens, *etc.* and I was told by the guard at the school gate to catch a bus to go downtown. Stepping up into the bus, I saw the sign "Colored in Rear." Calming myself down, I counted the number of bench-seat rows and sat down exactly halfway, feeling satisfied and non-controversial. This way, I would be safe either as a white, or a colored.

Since then, my perception of things around me has changed considerably—the whole world has changed considerably—and I remember these same inscribed words with mixed feelings, uncomfortable and even a little indignant at times. For I believe that our perception of God and our religious experience are deeply and intimately personal, seldom—if ever—completely confided to or candidly shared with other persons. In contrast, the government establishment is communal and of public domain, on the one hand, and utterly impersonal and quite temporal, on the other. And whenever I see or sense anything that implies the joining of hands between religion and politics, or between clerics (the people of priestly caste) and men of the powerful ruling class, I could not help feeling uneasy. For, you see, whenever these two forces join hands together, the power this merger forges becomes almost invincible. One may say that the power of the Green is made mightier because it now bears the insignia of God.

Like sandcastles on the beaches, government comes and goes, and regimes and dynasties rise and fall. It is a fairly common occurrence throughout history, East and West, that people would rise up against their rulers, claiming that the rulers had lost the mandate of heaven to rule, and overthrow them. But I have yet to read about people rising up and revolting against their own religion. (Surely, people of different religions have fought and will continue to fight against each other, as we see today the world over. But that is another story.) And the cunning politicians know this well and, as history has given witness time and again, politicians would often put on clerical garb. Or, if this is not possible, the politicians would stand very close to those who wear the garb. Religious leaders are certainly no one's fool either, and they know that they have something those politicians want. So the two join hands and forces, or at least politely exchange their approval, mutual support, and commodities, when doing so would be mutually beneficial: haloes over the political power.

It may be a surprise to realize how many wars have been declared in the name of god, with the pronouncement of clerics with the blessings of the church. And when a war is declared with the sanction of god or his earthly representative, the consequence is enormous and the disaster horrific. For the confused masses, even sensing that there may be something amiss, could only blindly follow the call to obey, for fear that, if they defy the divine order, their wretched souls may be forever damned by god, or his agents, those self-appointed spokesmen for the divine.

To be sure, the call to holy wars is not of recent invention, or contemporary phenomenon such as we have been seeing daily, vividly played out in nearly all parts of the world but particularly in the Middle Eastern regions: the *Jihad*, or "Holy War." There are tales after tales of holy wars in the Old Testament, the massacre of men, women, children and even cattle, all in the name of god, and claimed to be so ordered by god. Even closer to our time, we can find examples of jihad in the story of the Crusaders, who marched to reclaim Jerusalem, the "City of Peace," believed not only by the Jews but also Christians and Muslims to be the center—or the navel—of the entire world. The *jihad* of Crusades was called by the warrior Pope, Urban the Second. In calling the faithful to arms, Urban boldly claimed that "God willed it" and, thereby, transformed the countless meek pilgrims to vengeful crusading murderers of the believers of the same Father Abraham.

The sad truth is that it was actually far from what *God had willed*. It was not even for any true religious convictions on the part of this Pope, or any justifiable cause for the Church. Rather, it was conceived as a convenient way to divert attention from the current and mounting problems within the Church, the corruption on the part of the clerics (e.g., monks were getting rich from the sale of Penitence, the guarantee of salvation and promise of eternal life, all for the right price), and the power struggles and fierce divisions within the church polity. Beautiful and romantic tales of later creation about the Crusaders aside, many of the bands of Crusaders were in fact no better than roaming bandits, and there were even the so-called Crusaders who plundered villages of Christian dwellers, taking whatever they could and killing any living souls on sight, including, as the stories have it, roasting babies over open fires.

All these—including countless indescribable atrocities—were committed in the name of "purifying the earth for God." And what was the net result? Nothing much, really, except perhaps the fantastic tales of the mysterious East that the returning Crusaders brought home with them to the West. And they indeed had brought things of unequivocal proof that they were actually *there*, in the mysterious East: silk, perfume and spices. And the West was in its greedy element, and the Church and the likes of Marco Polo could hardly suppress their urge to conquer the East, east of Jerusalem, the farther east the better. And all this, actually, was the historical background that had fanned the fever of the likes of Marco Polo and Christopher Columbus to reach and reap the East.

O, the greed of man for power and for wealth. And when the greed for both power and wealth was satisfied, man not only would be king but also would be god. When power goes to the head, the swollen head begins to fantasize and makes man into believing that he is no longer a mortal but a god, or a virtual god. The tower of Babel is everywhere, visible or invisible, in every age. Caesars and Pharaohs had believed that they would become god when—or even before—they died and, today, the common people can still view in awe and worship the immortalized remains of Stalin and Mao Tzedong as if they are demigods. The history of man has witnessed time and again that, in those moments of feeling self-exaltation and aggrandizement, even the common man would begin to think that he is in some way specially endowed, that he is a descendant of gods or a super race, chosen by god and, thus, superior to all others. Hitler believed in the race of the Aryans, the race to which he and his followers belonged, and was a chosen of God. And he was destined, ordained, to found a *third* empire, after the two earlier empires (the Greek and the Roman), and this *Third Reich* was to endure for a thousand years.

Of the Far-Eastern countries, the Japanese claimed that their emperors were the direct descendants of *kami*, or gods, and their country was a *Shin-Koku*, Divine Nation. Truly, the throne of *bansei ikkei* (ten thousand generations, one lineage) had lasted longer than any empire in human history, so the Japanese believed. I can still recall the excitement of the festival scenes I witnessed as a mere lad, the occasion of the national jubilation of "*Kigen Nisen Roppiaku Nen*" (The 2600 Anniversary of the Founding of the Nation of Japan). And the Japanese have two chronicles to "prove" the authenticity of their claim of one lineage through ten thousand generations: the *Kojiki* and *Nihon Shoki* (even if they were committed to writing in the early eighth century, from oral tradition which was of much more ancient origin). The orthodox patriotic Japanese, though few in number these days, would still maintain that the present emperor is of the direct blood lineage of Japan's first emperor, the god-king Jimmu Tenno, regarding it as an indisputable historical fact. This may be likened to the claim of direct lineage from Adam to Abraham to David and Solomon to Jesus. And we have the Bible to prove it.

During World War II and, most probably in an attempt to counter the beliefs of Christians in Japan, Korea and Taiwan during those warring years, the Japanese (military) government resurrected the notion that their emperor was an *ara-hito gami* (god appearing in man's image), quite similar to the concept of "emanu-El"—god indwelling in man, and it was for this divine emperor that Japanese soldiers gave their lives willingly, joyfully and proudly.

I can remember the somber feeling that I, even as a child, had in watching small formations of Japanese fighter planes, usually four to six, rarely more, flying over the small mountain villages of our temporary "evacuation" dwelling, heading into the eastern sky toward the sea. It was often in the gray evening hours, and my sisters and I, sometimes with a few friends, would lift and cup our hands and bow our heads toward these planes in silent prayer. For we were told that these were the *kamikaze* planes, piloted by youthful airmen in their late teens and early twenties, making their life's final flight in rendezvous with death. (*Kamikaze* literally means "divine winds," and was the name the grateful—and much relieved—Japanese called the gale wind believed as *god-sent* to devastate the mighty Mongol navy that had entered the harbors of Japan. The winds and waves sent thousands of Khan's fierce warriors to the bottom of the sea.)

As children, we were told and had believed that Japanese soldiers and particularly those young and gallant *kamikaze* pilots, often the best among the fighter plane airmen, regarded this special assignment as the highest honor that could be bestowed on Japanese men of arms, and were most happy—even jubilant—to give their lives for their emperor-god. These planes were filled with only enough fuel for a one-way flight (so not to waste precious gasoline), just to reach and rendezvous with the targets of their suicidal mission—the US naval convoy. Just before they took off, the pilots would line up for the last word of instruction and blessing, and were given a drink of wine called *muku-no sake* ("untarnished wine") which in reality was pure water. Then these *kamikaze* pilots would recite, just before boarding their planes for the final flight of their life, a song set to an ancient patriotic poem, "*Umi Yuka Ba*." The verse goes like this:

> "*Umi yukaba, mizuku kabane,*
>   *yama yukaba, kusa musu kabane.*
> *O-Gimi no heni koso shi name,*
>   *kaheri mi wa seji.*"

> [To fight in the sea, my body shall be afloat amidst the waves,
>   To fight in the hills, my body shall rot amidst the grasses.
> Though I may die at the feet of my Great Lord,
>   I shall never look back (*i.e.*, I shall never regret).]

Fanatic? Pathetic? Senseless? Even hateful? Most certainly! Yet this was the kind of patriotism girded with religious conviction, the most powerful and dreaded sort of loyalty, when all senses were suppressed and benumbed under the zeal for their god. And there isn't much difference between the Japanese suicidal pilots reciting this patriotic poem, and the zealots of the ancient Jews who would rather die than break the laws of the Sabbath, or the Muslim *jihadeans* who willingly blow up their bodies with the shout of "***ALLAH IS GREAT!***"

It was one of the saddest days in the history of modern Japan. Two days after the atomic bombs were dropped, one in Hiroshima earlier and then another in Nagasaki, the voice of Emperor Hirohito was heard all over Japan, in the first-ever live radio broadcast of *Arahito*

Gami, the "God in Human Form." Millions of Japanese knelt before their radios, eyes closed and heads bowed low, many with their hands held in propitiation. "*Mattaku mottai nai*" ("completely too much grace to bear"); elder men and women, even the younger ones, sobbed uncontrollably. Like millions of Japanese, I also was hearing the voice of the Emperor for the first time. His voice was soft and even a little high pitched, and his speech deliberate but faltering. I did not understand all of what was being said, for his language was not the ordinary, conversational sort. But even an eleven year old knew, or could feel, that something very grave was being announced. My brother-in-law explained to us children in the simplest term, that the Emperor had just announced that Japan was surrendering to the Americans. My minister father appeared somber and motionless, but I could sense that there was a profound peace in his heart. I knew that he would no longer have to contend with the issue of the God of his faith and Japan's emperor whom we were forced to accept as divine and as the "incarnate of god."

The very next day, hundreds of people, mostly men, and many wearing their military uniforms or black formal traditional attire, gathered at the broad front courtyard of the Imperial Palace. There, they knelt down on the white gravel, facing the *Niju-Bashi* (the "Double-decked" Bridge), the arched stone bridge over which the emperor would occasionally appear, always riding his white horse, in order to grant his royal subjects a rare glimpse of their Lord. And there, on this front imperial courtyard, many military and ex-military men committed *seppuku* (or *harakiri*, suicide by self-inflicting dis-embowelment) This was the most honorable thing to do. For the defeat of war and national humiliation were already too much to bear, but now the *demythologizing* of their emperor-god was worse than the fate they chose. They had believed that their nation was endowed by heaven, their people specially chosen by the divine, and their emperor was the descendant of god. But, now, the emperor himself had disavowed his divinity. In their collective patriotic mind, with death only could they atone for this national humiliation.

We may wonder why Japanese people would possess such a fanatic devotion to their emperor-god, and regard it completely incomprehensible that zealots of the Muslim faith would not hesitate to blow themselves up while murdering innocent civilians in the same act. But it is a historically proven fact that such a total devotion always accompanies warfare when religion and politics become inseparably joined together, when war is regarded as an act "willed by god" who at the same time promises a far richer reward for the martyred jihad warriors in their afterlife: gold, land, maiden, or whatever one fancies in life. I suppose that, so long as humans are what they are, predisposed to greed, there will always be warfare. But the most horrid warfare, one that is abomination to God, is one that is fought "in the name of God," whether that god is *Allah*, *Kami*, or *Yahweh*.

One particular aspect about this is that I really could not recall reading or hearing about the emperor-god in any dynasties in China's long historical past. Emperors were called *tian-zhi*, the son of heaven. The emperor represents god in ruling the land, but never as god himself, and no Chinese emperor had ever fought his neighboring kingdom "in the name of god." This is probably why the Chinese people always have the moral mandate to overthrow an emperor when his reign is seen as not in the heavenly will. For the heavenly "son-ship" can be disowned and disavowed, just like a son can be cut off from inheritance if he is proven unworthy. When an emperor proves himself unworthy, the people will rise up and dethrone him "in the name of heaven" and give the throne to a more worthy person. This, in fact, was the fundamental concept behind the changes and successions of the imperial throne in China's historical past. We can even liken this ideal to the office of the U.S. presidency with an oath to uphold the Constitution. The Constitution remains fundamentally stable while the presidency changes hands, and when the man in the office is deemed unfit or unable to uphold the Constitution, he could be impeached or, in Chinese terms, "dethroned."

To be sure, there actually WAS a Chinese emperor who would be god, and he tried awfully hard. And for a while, it even appeared that he was going to get his wishes. This was *Qin Xi Huangdi* (pronounced *Chin-Shi Huang-Di*), the first true emperor—*Huangdi*—of China (2nd century B.C.E.), as opposed to *wang* or regional king. Even as a wang, he already had his eyes on all neighboring kingdoms and, in order to consolidate his power base, he systematically eliminated all the neighboring territories, killed their rulers and massacred the populace. Next, in order to make certain that no opposing opinion would ever be raised to disturb the "peace," he imprisoned and even buried alive intellectuals who were in any way suspect of mutiny in thoughts, words, or writings. And, for good measure, he had ordered that any and all suspected books be burned. He also turned to securing the borders of his now greatly expanded empire and, in an attempt to minimize the threats of invasion of the northern tribes (the famous *Xiungnus* who, centuries later, were dreaded by the Europeans as the *Huns* and, still later, settled in the present *Hung*aria), Emperor Qin Xi mobilized the entire country to undertake one of the greatest construction projects in human history. This was the building of the Great Wall(s), which was accomplished by extending and reinforcing the existing defensive walls, and connecting them all to form one, continuous Great Wall.

He was a visionary ruler. He built canals and highways, with all the highways being of the same width so that his military chariots could travel to all regions within his empire. He unified the systems of measurement and writing, and he collected all the weapons from the populace, and built himself a gigantic statute, just like the Babylonian king Nebuchadnezzar had done before him, and Stalin after him. Still uneasy, he established a system of civic and criminal law that was one of the most severe in human history: "*mieh jiou-zuh*." Under this penal code, if a criminal is found guilty, his entire clan to the "*ninth-degree kins would be put to death.*" (This penal code remained in China for nearly two millennia.)

Then, with all the earthly and political concerns properly and securely disposed of, he proclaimed himself "The First Emperor" (*Xi Huangdi*) of China. Wholly content, he then turned his attention to that which was the very attribute of gods: immortality. He sought far and wide for the dwelling place of gods, in order that he might obtain the potion that would give him everlasting life. Don't you see, when a politician has an all-consuming desire, he will always find a way. When the mighty lets it be known that he has a need, there always will be a priest or preacher who stands ready to offer a prayer for divine accommodation.

And, indeed, there was exactly such a "man of god," a taoist monk by the name of Xü Fu. This 'Reverend' Xü submitted to the throne that he indeed knew the dwelling place of gods, on an island in the eastern sea, from where the sun rose every morning. Emperor Qin Xi was ecstatic, and commanded Rev. Xü to make inquiry of the gods on the terms for obtaining the elixir of everlasting life. Rev. Xü went to the eastern sea, and returned to the throne with the following message: the gods would indeed grant the wishes of the emperor, with the offering of five thousand young men and five thousand young maidens of excellent physical and intellectual attributes.

The emperor thought that truly was a bargain. Wouldn't you, if you were the mightiest emperor and the uncontested master of all the wealth of the land, including the life and fate of all the people living under your oversee? Besides, ten thousand young people is nothing; "There are simply too many Chinese, anyway!" (I didn't say this; Premier Deng Xiaoping did, when he sent out the soldiers of his *People's Army* to crush—and massacre—those rowdy college students camped out in front of the "*Gate of Heavenly Peace*"—the *Tian'An Men* square, shouting "Long live democracy!")

So the emperor had ten thousand of the finest young men and maidens selected, in accordance with the terms of the offering, and he even provided the Reverend with all he needed for the long voyage, plus a sizable amount of gold and silver, as a gesture of gratitude from this absolute ruler of the land. For, as a politician, Emperor Qin Xi knew very well that gods and their agents were easily ingratiated by a little extra offering of gold and silver.

And Rev. Xü set sail toward that eastern island in the direction of the *rising sun*, with the full precious cargoes. That was the last time the Emperor or anyone in his dominion saw Rev. Xü and the ten thousand youths, not to mention all the gold and silver that went aboard—and abroad—with the man of god.

If this tale was true, one may wonder where had Rev. Xü and the ten thousand fine young people of the Qin dynasty gone. They certainly couldn't have gone very far. Had they gone far, far away, as Columbus did some seventeen centuries later, they could have been the first to reach the American Continent and, then, who knows, Chinese might have become the official language of the United States a couple of millennia later. (Some wishful thinking! But, the truth is, the Chinese did reach the American Continent long *before* Columbus, on the far northern shore. Perhaps you will be interested in reading Gavin Menzies' book titled *1421: THE YEAR CHINA DISCOVERED AMERICA* (pub. 2002) to know that I am not making all this up.)

No, they didn't get that far; they didn't even reach Hawaii. What the legend does suggest is that the convoy of ships did arrive on the islands in the ocean east of China's northeastern coast, in the direction of the rising sun, in the land of what is now Japan. And it appeared that the convoy made a few stopovers on the southwestern coasts of Korea. The more recent archaeological finds provide evidence to the truthfulness of at least part of the legend of Taoist monk Xü Fu and his army of ten thousand youths. There, as the legend goes, Rev. Xü Fu proclaimed himself the *first* emperor (possibly Japan's legendary first, true human emperor Jimmu?) of that newfound kingdom, where his loyal subjects of ten thousand healthy, intelligent and handsome youths served him obediently. And, together, they lived happily ever after.

Poor Emperor Qin Xi! No wonder he was so hopping mad that he had ten thousand life-size and life-like terra cotta soldier figures made, complete with horses and chariots and with real weapons in their hands, to stand guard in his imperial tomb, just in case he found himself resurrected and had to start fulfilling his imperial dreams all over again. (Actually, the terra cotta soldier figures were created because the emperor could not bear the thought of having his royal guard buried alive with him, as the ritual dictate of the day required. He was a warrior emperor and had fought with these royal guards of his side by side in many battles. As to his many wives and concubines, however, he felt no need to extend the same regards. And, so, the empresses and consorts were all summarily entombed alive with him, all proper and official, in accordance with the dictate of the royal ritual custom.)

We would never know what thoughts had gone through the head of this First Emperor of China when he was lying on his deathbed. It is quite possible that he was consumed with anger and remorse, and swore to heaven that, if indeed he should find himself resurrected, he wouldn't be fooled into believing the likes of the taoist monk. Instead, he just might go to one of those Television Evangelists who would always promise over the airwaves the healing power, health, success and a richly rewarding and *everlasting life*, in exchange for a small donation. And this first emperor of China will certainly have enough hard dough (*terra cotta* is dough, you know, very hard *clay dough*) to more than satisfy any TV preacher's plea for donation, or *dough*-nation.

Praise the Lord, and pass the offering plate. And a promise of immortality for a price, preferably the kind on which is inscribed [**IN GOD WE TRUST**].

6

The Mystery of the 'Rising Sun'

It would indeed seem that the tale of this cunning taoist monk Xü Fu and his ten thousand youths reaching the islands of Japan and establishing a new nation, afar from the wicked reign of Qin Xi Huangdi, and eventually becoming the present nation of Japan a couple of millennia later, is highly improbable and even absurd. Regardless of its probable truthfulness in history, and whether the people of this modern island nation were seeded by this taoist monk and his youthful followers, or by some other tribal migrants during the course of centuries in the prehistoric period, there is little doubt that Japan, Korea, and China are related archaeologically and culturally.

It is a well-known fact that, for example, before the last ice age, there was a land bridge between Asia and the present Alaska, and early man had migrated from Asia to the North American continent for many centuries long before Columbus "discovered" the New World. Archaeologists and anthropologists can map out the migratory routes of ancient people all over the world, and there isn't much dispute about the origin of the Chinese people, or Indian people, for example. But, somehow, the history of the origin of the Japanese people is still shrouded in mystery, even today with all its scientific knowledge. Scientists aren't all that sure, indeed downright uncertain, about where the proto-Japanese people came from, and there are still more questions than answers. For example, on the island of Hokkaido, the northernmost in the Japanese archipelago, there lives an uniquely distinct tribe known as Ainu, and this people has no known ethnological anthropological link to any known stock of the Asian race, Mongolians, Chinese or even Japanese. There are many books that present different views on where the proto-Japanese people had come from. Some base their argument on linguistic elements, others on the evidence of archaeological finds, and still others on some peculiar customs such as religious rites and cultic practices that are wholly unique to the Japanese people. The more recent DNA genetic research studies even support the theory that the Japanese people are more closely related to the Middle-Eastern people, and not to China's main tribe, the Han people.

Fascinated by this subject, I even ventured to offer (as a part of my doctoral dissertation) an additional perspective to this question of the origin of the Japanese people, by way of an analytical comparative study of traditional music, and attempted to provide evidence that traditional musical traits of the Japanese people are fundamentally different from those of the Chinese. Therefore, to me, the very notion that this taoist monk Xü Fu was the first emperor of Japan, or that his ten thousand healthy, handsome and intelligent youths were the ancestors of the modern Japanese people, is simply preposterous. If it were so, then our big Jewish friend who believed that Japanese and Chinese are all the same would be correct, and then our little Chinese friend would never again dare to go to the Jewish delicatessen to enjoy a lunch of kosher corn-beef sandwich, and that would be a downright shame.

But, on this matter, and to make my case a bit more convincing, I should do a bit more explaining.

First, the dating is quite wrong. There is a rather credible historical chronology (excluding the early mythological tales) that dates Japan's history back to about twenty-six and half centuries, and archaeological evidence (for example, the *jomon* terra cotta unearthed in various parts of Japan) predates even this period by a few millennia. But this particular topic is somewhat specialized and any discussion of it would require a fair amount of archaeological information and, therefore, we should perhaps not pursue this any further here.

Second, the difference in one of the most important tools of civilization is so great between the Japanese and Chinese people that they could not have come from the same cultural origin: the *written* language. While the Chinese had written language as long as three to four thousand years ago, the Japanese people did not possess any written language until about the third to fourth century by adopting Chinese writing. However, this borrowing of China's system of written language caused an insurmountable problem and confusion (see below). Subsequently, in the ninth century, Japan had finally created its own system of writing, essentially a system of alphabet (like all European languages), fundamentally differing from the ideographic and pictographic writing of the Chinese people (which most closely parallels the writing of the ancient Sumerians—the *cuneiform*, and the Egyptians—the *hieroglyphics*). One may even venture to say that the two fundamental principles of writing are: (1) the pictorial and idea-connoting, to which Chinese, Egyptian and Sumerian scripts belong, and (2) the phonetic symbols of the alphabet, to which the ancient Phoenicians, Greek and Roman and all subsequent European and Indo-European scripts belong.

Third, and one of the most important clues, is that the *spoken* language is all wrong. That is, the Chinese and Japanese speak two *fundamentally different languages*, and the difference is far more than the difference between, say, English and German or French. Certainly, the modern Japanese language contains many linguistic elements of Chinese (but not *vice versa*). For instance, the pronunciation of some written words in these two languages is quite similar and even identical at times, since all Japan's *kanji* are borrowed and adopted from China (*kan-ji* literally means the written words of the *Han* people, pronounced as *Kan* in Japanese). But the *fundamental* difference, still existing between the two languages of these neighboring countries even after coexisting, communicating, exchanging, and fighting off and on for some two millennia, can best be explained as below:

> Chinese spoken language is *monosyllabic* and *tonal,*
>   *versus*
> Japanese spoken language is *polysyllabic* and *non-tonal.*

Explanation, please.

'Mono-syllabic' means that each word has only one syllable, like *ren* (man, person), *jia* (house), *ma* (horse). This contrasts to 'poly-syllabic' which means that each word (nearly always) has two or more syllables, like *hito* (man, person), *i-ye* (house), *uma* (horse). This polysyllabic reading of otherwise Chinese written word—often referred to as character—is a lingering of the traditional, even archaic manner of speech of the Japanese people. At the same time, the modern Japanese could also read these same characters cited here *after Chinese pronunciation,* *mono*syllabically, as *jin* (man), *ka* (house), and *ba* (hose). The Japanese linguists refer to the first, more archaic, polysyllabic manner of reading and speaking as Old Japanese (OJ), and to the second, more recent (beginning in about the sixth century), Chinese style monosyllabic manner of reading and speaking as New Japanese (NJ).

The difference is not limited to polysyllabic *versus* monosyllabic. The syntax, grammar and word order are also fundamentally different. In fact, the traditional Japanese is more closely related to the Tibetan language and even as far west as to the archaic Turkish language.

Then, there is the matter of tones, or inflections. Tonal inflection is somewhat like short 'musical' contour, with voice ending going up, going down, holding even, or short staccato. European languages do have tones, but they are not a requisite in distinguishing the word meaning. The tones in the Western languages are referred to as 'accent' and are articulated in terms of long, short (called *agogic* accent), or strong, weak (called *dynamic* accent). In the monosyllabic language such as Chinese, the tonal inflection becomes critically important, because the slightest change in tonal inflection on a monosyllabic sound would completely alter the meaning of the word. In Mandarin (the official language of China, also called *putong hua*), for example, there are four tones: even, up, down, short. Applying these different inflection to a monosyllabic sound of MA, for example: 'MA' may mean "mother" (with the even tone), "grass fibre" (with the uplifting tone), "horse" (with the downturn tone), or "scold" (with short staccato). And certainly you wouldn't want to get your "mother" and the "horse" mixed up.

There were, until the end of World War II, some two hundred distinctively different dialects in China, the difference caused primarily by the different tonal inflections on the same words among different dialects. The only way Chinese could communicate with one another between people of different provinces was by writing, and this is still true between Chinese living in China and the overseas Chinese, many of them descendants of southern provinces and thus still clinging to their ancestral dialects.

When Japanese began to engage Chinese *written* language to write out their own *spoken* language during the sixth to eighth centuries (when Buddhism first entered Japan through Korea), it created an insurmountable problem. How could the Japanese use the monosyllabically pronounced Chinese characters (which also employ tonal inflections) to represent the sounds of the Japanese language (which are polysyllabic and non-tonal)? Moreover, each Chinese character connotes specific meaning, while each syllable in Japanese spoken language connotes nothing specific.

The Chinese written language entered Japan around the (late) fifth century, with the introduction of Buddhism from China and through Korea. When Buddhism became popular and even embraced by the members of the imperial court, the orthodox Japanese (the imperial court in particular) felt that their traditional belief (*shintoism*) was threatened. Thereby the imperial court felt that a document that would provide credence to the history of their ancestors, handed down for countless generations as mythological tales, must be produced. There was a problem, however. These mythological tales were transmitted orally. They had never been written down.

Therefore, in 722, the imperial court commissioned the first official chronicle of Japan to be written, and the result was *Kojiki* (*The Record of Ancient Affairs*). The chronicle was written entirely with Chinese characters, and each of the polysyllabic names in ancient mythologies was thereby written out with several Chinese characters. Thus began a process of *misreading* on immense scale, creating thereby a nearly insoluble problem even for the modern scholars of historical anthropology.

There is, for example, the name of the land from where the mythological deities had descended, called '*Hi-taka-mi no kuni*,' written out with four Chinese characters to mean "Sun-High-View Country." But recent scholarship (especially after the War) has ascertained that this reading (into the meaning as connoted in the Chinese characters) is entirely erroneous. The more correct reading, the scholars hold, is "*kita-kami no kuni*" which can be written out with three Chinese characters, to more accurately mean "the country (or the land) up north." Scholars call such erroneous use and reading of Chinese characters (hence producing erroneous meaning) "*ate-ji*" (literally, *word to fit* [the sound, rather than to properly connote the meaning]).

It was for this reason that the imperial house and the populace saw the need to create a system of writing which is capable of representing Japanese spoken language without the encumbrance of Chinese connotation with each monosyllable sound. The result was the system of *kana* (literally means "false name"), taking certain parts of Chinese characters as a phonetic symbol. It is essentially an alphabet system where each symbol would represent a phonetic sound, without any connoted meaning. There are even two *kana* systems, one called *kata-kana* (*partial* false name), while the other called *hira-gana* (*fluid-script*(ed) false name).

To be sure, all the alphabet systems currently in use had grown out of much earlier pictographic or ideographic systems of writing. The alphabet system of all the European countries—including the one used in the Soviet Union—also had its origin in the Phoenician alphabet system that came from a simplified version of an even earlier pictographic script. Taking, for example, the letter A. The modern letter A was an upside-down picture of the head of a cow, and the word for cow in the Phoenician language was *alf* (or *alef*). What was initially a drawing of a cow's head was turned upside down (in the upper-case letter A) or sideway (in the lower-case letter *a* or as in Greek alphabet letter for *A*) and was identified as a single phonetic sound of "ah," no longer connoting or resembling a cow's head.

In quite a similar fashion, the Japanese took parts of Chinese pictographic and ideographic symbols—the characters—and formulated their own system of alphabet, no longer having any connoted meaning of the original Chinese characters. To be sure, Japanese continued to employ Chinese characters in connoting the original meaning of the word. These Chinese characters are called "the *ji* (letters) of *Kan* (or

Han, i.e, the *Han* Dynasty, lasting from the third century B.C.E. to the third century C.E., one of the most powerful and influential dynasties in China's history). The Japanese writing today is a mixture of Chinese characters and the letters of their own alphabet system, even mixing both the *kata-kana* and *hira-gana* for emphasis or supplemental notation.

Japan, in fact, was so earnest in learning from China and subscribing to China's system of government, education, and societal codes, including the legal and moral laws, that for a few centuries around the tenth century the Japanese government sent the official envoy—the *ken-to shi* (scholars sent to *To, i.e. Tang* dynasty)—to study and transmit all things Chinese. Soon, the ability to read, to write and recite Chinese poetry and literary works was regarded as the mark of the educated and of high social caste, even including the samurai class (especially after the mid-seventeenth century, after the battle of *Seki-ga Hara* was fought and the first true *shogunate* was established to rule over the entire Japan). From this, too, the Chinese pronunciation of written characters was beginning to get incorporated more and more into Japanese spoken language, even the daily conversation of the common folks.

The Japanese did not totally abandon their own spoken language, however, and the result was the coexistence of two entirely different systems of pronouncing nearly everything: the OJ (old Japanese) and NJ (new Japanese). We can illustrate this by showing two different ways of counting numbers:

> (For illustration, the Taiwanese dialect is chosen to represent the Chinese pronunciation of numbers. The linguistic scholars believed that Taiwanese dialect had originally come from northeast China, quite close to Japan, and had changed little over the centuries, as it was preserved in an isolated island of Taiwan. The origi-

nal people speaking the dialect were exiled from their homeland when their region was defeated and forced to exile down south, and eventually settled in Taiwan. In the romanized pronunciation illustration, a superscript "n" indicates a nasal sound, as in "knee."

Arabic numeral	Chinese	New Japanese	Old Japanese
1	it (or chit)	ichi	hito(-tsu)
2	ji (or nng^n)	ni	futa(-tsu)
3	sam (or sa^n)	san	mi(-ttsu)
4	shih (or suh)	shih	yo(-ttsu)
5	go^n	goh	itsu(-tsu)
6	lyok (or lak)	loku	mu(-ttsu)
7	chit	shichi	nana(-tsu)
8	pat (or peh)	hachi	ya(-ttsu)
9	kyu (or kau)	kyu	kokono(-tsu)
10	ship (or tzap)	jyu	toh

Should you attempt to pronounce these Japanese numbers (or all Japanese words) properly, make sure you enunciate every syllable (as in reading Italian), each nearly equal in duration (no funny Texas drawl, please). If in doubt, speak it evenly, as in a monotone voice, making certain that all the vowels are in Italian pronunciation (open, bright and pure vowel sound). Thus A is "ah" (as in fAther); I is "ee" (as in Inn or "feet"); U is "oo" (as in Ukulele or "noodle"); E is "eh" (as in End or "bet"); and O is "oh" (as in "Oh!" and "So!").

Hence, *shogun* is to be correctly pronounced as shOH-gOOn" (and not sho-GUN), and *karaoke* should be enunciated as "kAH-rAH-OH-kEH" (the word literally means "empty orchestra" where *kara* as in "*kara-te*" of martial arts, and *oke* is an abbreviation of *OH-kesu-tora* (for orchestra.).

Of course we know that *kara-oke* originated in Japan, for singing to the accompaniment of "canned" music. The accompaniment of the "absent orchestra" gave birth to naming of a form of entertainment created by business people or office workers of Japan. After a day's hard work in the stifling office where everyone pretends to be so serious, the psychologically drained men would descend on the neighborhood bar. After a few (or more than a few) drinks, their inhibition now diluted by *sake* and their ingrained sense of social propriety completely overcome by the spirit (you know, the *chemical* kind), these men would let out or, more accurately, *belt out* what is remotely resembling singing, in a crazed and comical imitation of pop singers. It is an art form of unparalleled originality that only the Japanese could invent. We may suppose it also has a considerable medicinal benefit, in ridding the pressures of life and work, and restoring a sense of normalcy and equilibrium. It is downright shameful of national proportion, therefore, when Americans would so blatantly and ignominiously *mis*pronounce the name of this most characteristic Japanese *art*(?!) form, as something close to *keri-oki* (almost sounding like *ketsu-oke* which, alas, may mean either "*bloody bucket*" or even "*buttom bucket*"). It is in times like this that I wonder if average Americans know how to properly pronounce the basic vowel sounds associated with the letters A, E, I, O, and U.

On the other hand, to speak Chinese properly, with correct tonal inflection, the task is of entirely a different sort. It even has a keen 'musical' sense of hearing as prerequisite to distinguish the finely differentiated tonal contours. Mandarin (the official Chinese language which in fact was a 'dialect' of the area of the capital Beijing and thus regarded as the courtly language) engages four tonal inflections, but my Taiwanese dialect has eight, and the Cantonese dialect (as spoken in Hong Kong) has nine. But, even with only four inflections, the acquiring of proficiency in the Chinese spoken language poses a formidable task. It might be noted that this difficulty presents itself not only to foreigners but also to fellow Chinese from different provinces. For example, the phrase "How much is a bowl of soup dumplings (*shui-jiau yi-wan doshao chian*)?" might be quite erroneously understood by another Chinese from a different province as "How much is one-night sleeping (with you) (*shui-jiau yi-wan doshao chian*)?" Of course, tonal language is frustratingly difficult particularly for Americans who are not known to be good with foreign languages.

One particular Monday morning many years ago, my brother-in-law, who was the local director of an American missionary correspondence office in Taiwan (the headquarters, the office of TEAM, in Wheaton, IL) noticed that one American missionary lady looked pensive, even disturbed. Upon his inquiry, she confided that she was at a loss, and concerned that she might somehow have offended the Chinese lady next door. "All I wanted was to borrow some glue, but she became very angry," she said. She explained that, late Saturday night while she was preparing the flannel board for her Sunday school lessons, she ran out of glue, and went next door to borrow some from the lady whom she had befriended only recently. But the lady became agitated and infuriated, and said something loud in Chinese, and slammed the door in her face, and she simply couldn't figure out why. My brother-in-law sensed that perhaps it was the way she said it that was not quite right, and asked the distraught missionary to repeat *exactly* what she had said.

"I said, '*Wo koh pu-koh yi jieh ni deh jiang-fuh mah?*'"

My brother-in-law burst out in roaring laughter. "You actually said to this lady, 'May I borrow your husband?'" You see, in Chinese, glue is *jiang-fu* (*fu* in the third inflection), while husband is *zhang-fu* (*fu* in the first inflection).

How do you think a self-respecting Chinese lady would react when, in the middle of a humid summer night, an American lady, wearing her near-see-through nightgown, suddenly appearing at your door steps, asked if she could borrow your husband?

The answer:

You would let out a few, well-chosen Chinese words of righteous indignation, and slam the door in the face of this alien female.

7

The Mystery of the Lost Sacred Relics

My almost-five-year-old son Geoffrey reminds me so much of myself in many ways. When he is good, I am doubly proud that he is so much like me, and I even entertain myself with a heart-warming thought that he inherited all that from me. But there are times, too, that he is simply exasperating, and then I would hope my wife would not remind me of how much Geoffrey is like me when he is impossible.

One of his characteristic traits is that he never stops asking questions, and he once asked "Daddy, God made everything. Did God make mosquitoes, too?" Such questions were most often asked on Wednesday afternoon when I picked him up from pre-K class at First Baptist Church, Denton, the day when a chapel period was held in the morning and children were told of many wonderful stories about God and his creation. Then, on that particular day, his question had a *segue* part, a difficult part. "Daddy, *why* did God make mosquitoes?" I couldn't very well answer and say God created mosquitoes so they could bite bad people, because I have a dark complexion and warm body temperature, and I attract mosquitoes like they all know my name.

It was times like this that I thought back to my childhood days, and wondered how my Christian minister father answered all the impossible questions I used to put to him, about God and about Japanese mythological figures I learned at *sho-gakko* (primary school for Japanese children), questions such as "Do you know *Amaterasu O-MiKami* was the sun goddess, and the whole world would turn dark when she hid herself in the cave?" or "Who is greater, God (*i.e.*, the Christian God) or the Japanese emperor who is *ara-hito-gami*? ("god in human form;" as mentioned earlier, it connotes a concept quite similar to *Immanu-El* in Hebrew, "god dwelling in man").

The first of these questions mentioned above had to do with a wonderfully colorful tale from Japan's mythological past, and it goes something like this (in a greatly simplified version):

All the gods (*kami*) were having fun one day and there was laughter and singing, and drinking. (The Japanese men's love of *sake* is legendary, a habit no doubt inherited from their ancestral demigods. In other words, it is a case of "the *kami*—rather than the devil—made me do it!") And, after a while, they got really rowdy. (Japanese men still do, and they invented *kara-oke*—now you know how to pronounce it correctly—to make themselves even more silly.) Among the demigods was *Ama-terasu O-Mi Kami* (literally means the "Great Heaven-Illuminating God[dess]), the most revered of all demigods in Japanese mythology who was the source of light and life, who illuminated the entire cosmos with her radiance.

Then, one of the demigods—actually the very younger brother of the sun-goddess—played a very nasty practical joke on her (I won't go into detail here, not in print, anyway), which shamed and angered the great goddess. And she parted company with the bunch of drunken demigods and went inside a cave, and put a huge stone to block out any intruders. The whole creation turned dark immediately, and cocks began to crow. All the demigods, now sober, begged her to come out of hiding. But the goddess admantly refused.

Now, regaining their senses and recognizing the seriousness of the situation, the demigods devised a scheme to lure the goddess out of the cave. First, one female demigod stripped herself naked and tap-danced on an overturned tub (she became the world's first *tub-dancer*). All the demigods surrounded the nude dancer, and sang, hollered, clapped, stomped, and played drums, to "make a joyful **noise** unto the goddess," you see. (This was the forerunner of a much later Japanese invention with equal silliness: the *karaoke*.)

Goddess *Amaterasu* could not suppress her *curiosity*; after all, she is a *female*, even if she is a god(dess). What could those guys out there be celebrating when they didn't have my presence, and their world was in total darkness, she wondered? So, she rolled the rock a little, just enough to take a peek. Standing by the rock was a demigod of great strength, and he immediately pulled the huge granite away from the cave entrance. The radiant *Amaterasu* reemerged from the cave, and the whole world was again bathed in her radiance. And, again, the cock crowed.

These and other tales from Japan's mythological past are fascinating in a number of ways. For one thing, these gods and demigods behaved much like humans. They caroused, schemed, drank and got drunk. They loved (chasing goddesses and even stealing the wives of other gods) and hated, and they killed one another. In this respect, Japan's mythological tales are very much like the ancient Greek tales. But I must hasten and get back to the more important point in citing this particular story.

Here, Sun is personified as a female—a goddess. This is wholly UN-Chinese. To the Chinese, as well as many other ancient cultures, the Sun was always regarded as male or, in Chinese terms, represents the *Yang* spirit, while the Moon is female or the *Yin* spirit. Likewise, day is *yang*, and night is *yin*; fire is *yang* and water is *yin*, *etc*. Therefore, the fact that this Japanese mythological tale has the Sun represented by a female figure would seem to suggest that the source of the tale and the entire oral tradition may have its origin outside China.

One theory (proposed by the Japanese anthropologists and cultural historians) is that goddess Amaterasu represents a cult of sun-worship, and that the goddess was most likely a lead female shaman of this cult. Shamanism is widespread even today in Japan, Korea, and all northeast Asia (as well as Africa), and this theory has many proponents. But, while the word *O-Mikami* itself was clearly of Japanese origin meaning "great god(dess)," perhaps the more interesting point of inquiry is the hidden meaning in the name Amaterasu. For clearly, the character employed to represent the name was a much later *ateji* (see before), and the original significance in the phonetic sound *a-ma-te-ra-su* may very well have been lost forever in the course of oral transmission during many centuries.

As explained in another essay (see "The Mystery of the Rising Sun"), the Japanese did not possess any form of *written language of their own* (until about the ninth century), and all their historical and mythological tales were handed down from one generation to the next by oral tradition, all through the incredible memory recitation of the tribe's elder oraclers. When Chinese *characters* were adopted, the ideographic characters—the words, with specific meaning—were used as phonetic symbols, as if these characters are alphabet lettters, devoid of meaning. But when words were used as phonetic symbols, the inevitable occurred: the unwitting reading of meaning into the sound. For example, the phonetic sound of the word "categorize" can also be represented by connecting three words: CAT + EGO + RISE, and one may be tempted to read some meaning into this three-word-spelled. This sort of mis-reading or meaning-reading into a name, or, in Japanese, the *ateji*, occurred often in the course of deciphering ancient scripts. There is a famous example of this *ateji* in the Old Testament: the name of the *Red* Sea, which the Israelites crossed in the exodus from Egypt, was actually a misreading of "*reed* sea," a shallow waterway between Egypt and the Sinai Desert, where water plants or reeds grew in abundance.

It is quite possible, therefore, that the name *a-ma-te-ra-su* was never intended to mean "heaven illuminating." All we could ascertain is that the name connoted something that was related to sun worship. But, what, exactly?

Let us leave this scene for a moment, and shift our attention to the Near East, the part of the ancient world which, culturally and geographically speaking, lay halfway between ancient Greece (the *western* center of the known and highly civilized world) and China (the *eastern* center of another known and also highly civilized world), to the time when it is said that ancient "Japan" (the name came much, much later) was first founded (about twenty two to twenty-six centuries ago). We are referring to the vast region under the ancient Persian Empire (including present-day Iraq, Iran, Turkey, and all the adjacent regions in what we now call the Middle East). During this period, there flourished in the Persian Empire one dominant cult, a religious belief embraced by the majority of the common people, though not the official religion of Persia.

This was a sun-worshipping cult called *mythraism*, and the name of the chief deity was *Mithras*. This cult had lasted a considerable length of time, through the Greek and the following Roman periods. Through its cultic tradition, the worship of god Mythras was always officiated by the priestesses. And it is difficult for me not to venture a hypothesis that the *Mithras* cult of ancient Persia was in fact the precursor of the *a-Matherasu* cult of Japan, that the similarity or the near-exact parallel between the name *Mi-th-ras* and *a-Ma-te-rasu* was not simply a coincidence. (The initial vowel "a" in *A-ma-te-ra-su* can be explained as of common practice of adding this open vowel—often followed by an "L" to form AL or EL—to the name signifying its exalted status, be it of a person, a deity, a mountain, such as *Allah*, *Elohim*, *Alps*, and *altitude*, *etc.*)

Let us suppose, just for the moment, then, that this tale of *A-Materasu* (note the change in hyphenation) did come from the Near East, possibly from a region in Persia, one of the greatest of the ancient empires, preserved in the oral tradition of a splinter sect of Persia's mythraism. Could it be that the name of this and other personages in Japan's mythological tales had their origin in cults of the ancient Middle East and Central Asia? And are there any evidences to support such a theory?

We had mentioned that the old Japanese language is polysyllabic and non-tonal and thus is completely unrelated to the Chinese language. Linguists would even suggest that the OJ resembles more closely the Near-Eastern language (*e.g.*, the ancient Turkish language) in phonetics as well as in syntax and grammatical structure. If so, where could the proto-Japanese people have come from? For grammar and syntax alone do not a language or a people make.

I am not a linguist, and I certainly am not an anthropologist. And I am afraid I could not offer much else in these regards. But I do have a few more pieces of information—call them evidence or just peculiar historical and cultural tidbits—to offer. All I ask is that you keep an open mind. As the saying goes, truth can sometimes be stranger and more incredible than fiction.

In the first great historical chronicle of China, *Shih-Ji*, written during the Western Han Dynasty (2nd century, B.C.E.), there is a passage that appears rather ordinary, but perhaps significant enough to warrant an entry into the chronicle. The statement refers to a migrant tribe, coming from the west of China's border (along the newly established trade route later called the Silk Road), that continued their migratory journey eastward. The statement itself carries no particularly noteworthy information, for countless camel caravans traversed this first great "communication highway" between the northwestern provinces of China and the regions beyond the western slopes of the Himalayan ranges. There is, however, a curious "note" identifying this particular tribe: it was called by the chronicler as "the people of knife's cult." Historians had puzzled over this name, and wondered what was this people of the "knife's cult," whence they had come from, and thither had they gone after passing through the central plains region of China?

Coming from the west of China could only mean that they had come from the Near East region, and going to the east of China could only be to the Korean Peninsula and, crossing the relatively narrow strait of ocean, to the islands of Japan. But how about the "knife's cult" as the identifying mark of this people? This could not mean the use of a knife for animal sacrifice, for the Chinese themselves did—and still observe the—practice of animal sacrifice. Could this be a reference to the *ritual of circumcision* that all Semitic people held (and still regard) as one of the most important religious requisites?

In fact, one Jewish tribe or a travel group did settle in the central plains region of China, in the city of Keifen, though perhaps a few centuries after the migrant tribe that was recorded in *Shih Jih*. Scholars have provided unequivocal proof that, until a relatively recent past, the Jewish community in Kaifen still possessed a sacred copy of the *Torah* (apparently a re-copied edition, containing numerous errors). And it is an indisputable historical fact that Jewish migration from the Middle East to the Far Eastern regions had continued, even sporadically, for many, many centuries following the Roman period. Indeed these Jews were renowned trader merchants of silk and spices.

The cult of worshipping the sun-god *Mithras* within the region of the Persian Empire, *versus* A-*Materasu* as the sun goddess who probably was the chief priestess of the cult; the reference in the *Han chronicle* about an west-east migrating tribe during the Early (or the Western) Han dynasty who was identified as practicing the 'knife's cult," *versus* the probable date of the "founding" of the nation of *Yamato* (the older name for the central island of Japan), *etc.* If these and many other parallels (see below) are mere coincidence, they are just too *curiously coincidental.* But, before you say yea or nay, let me offer a few more "circumstantial" evidences.

On July 17 every year, various *shinto* shrines in Japan hold a religious festival called *Gion no Matsuri* (the Feast of Gion). At the conclusion of the seven-day festival, there is a parade of "*O-Mikoshi.*" This *O-Mikoshi* is a square sacred chest, with an ornate roof and, atop the roof, is a golden bird with widespread wings. The name *O-Mikoshi* literally means the "Divine [chest of] Witness" or "Sacred Promise," and is carried with two long side poles by eight (or more) men (but never by women). The bodies of men are bare to the waist, their foreheads with white head bands, and they dance wildly, moving forward, backward and sideways as if totally spellbound, all the while incesssantly and boisterously shouting "*wasshoi! wasshoi! wasshoi!*" Finally, the men, still carrying the Divine Chest, would wade into the waterway, river or ocean, waist or even chest deep but never letting the holy relic become submerged.

On newyear's eve, the devout *shinto* faithful would enter the sacred compound late at night, and gather in front of the shrine. The *shinto shrines* do not have any figures or otherwise visible images of deities. (This in comparison to *temples* where sculptured or painted figures of deities are always present and, hence, Buddhist *temples*.) I do remember that, as a schoolboy, I also had attended the newyear's eve ritual. In spite of the crowd, the ground is eerily quiet, with only the sound from people walking on the graveled ground, in semi-darkness where the only light was from the torch stands high above the crowd. Then, at the command of the officiating *kan-nushi* (*shinto* priest), each person would take a piece of paper precut in a figure of man. Each person would wipe his or her body, in a gesture of cleansing, and then toss the paper figure into the bonfire. This is an act of cleansing of sins of the year, and the burning of the paper figure as a ritual atonement of the sacrificial lamb, as it were.

One of the most sacred and revered of all *shinto* shrines in Japan is the Grand Ise Shrine (the *Ise Dai Jingu*), on the gentle hills of the city of Ise about an hour's train ride from the city of Nagoya which, in turn, is approximately midway between *Kyoto* (literally means the Capital City) and *Tokyo* (the "Eastern Capital"). The *Ise Shrine*, with about two millennia history, consists of many, many buildings large and small. But the main sanctuary consists of two shrines, the *Nai-gu* ("Inner" Shrine) and the *Ge-gu* (or *Ge-ku*, "Outer" Shrine). The *Ise* Shrine is specifically dedicated to the worship of the great sun-goddess *Amaterasu O-Mikami* and, hence, its greatest historical and ritualistic importance among all the *shinto* pantheon.

Reposed deep within the *Naigu*, the holy of holies of the Shrine, is an article of incredible mystery, called *MiFune Shiro*. The literal meaning of this name is "The Replica of Divine Boat." According to the available descriptions, this sacred article is a wooden chest of approximately seven feet in length (with the inner opening of a little over five feet), about two and a half feet in both width (inner width of two feet) and height (inner depth of about one foot and a half). According to tradition, this sacred chest contains three sacred relics, collectively called *san-po* ("three treasures").

There is a serious problem, however. There are only two articles, not three. And the references in various historical chronicles and documents (such as the imperial house record of sacred articles) more often than not mention two articles only: One is a sword, called *kusanagi no tsurugi*, a sword with three protruding blades on each side, thus together with the sword point, seven "branches" and, hence, also called *shichi-shi to* (seven branched sword). The other article is called *kangami* which is believed to be a bronze mirror.

Before I describe the significance of these two sacred relics, let me pause for a moment, and shift the scene of our story back to the Middle East, to the time of the ancient Israelites, from Moses to King Solomon, or, from the wilderness wandering to the building of the great Temple of Solomon. You may be getting a little jet-lag dizziness from all this jetting back and forth between the two ancient worlds. But bear with me, for the climax is yet to come. So, tighten your seat belt, and brace yourself. Because I am going to take you off to a realm of an incredible (or even unbelievable) twilight zone of history and, in the course, may even shake you up a little. I only ask that you will please keep an open mind.

Many of us are familiar with or remember hearing about the Old Testament story of the "Ark of the Lord" told from the Sunday pulpit. The Ark was the single most sacred article of the ancient Israelites, for inside the Ark was the testament of their faith, the tangible proof of the faithfulness of their God Yahweh (or Jehovah, which is now believed to be an incorrect pronunciation of the consonant letters in spelling the name of God). This holy receptacle was held as signifying God's promise to dwell among His people Israel, and to act on their behalf. Hence it is called the Ark of the *Covenant*, also variously called the Ark of *Witness*, the Ark of *Promise*, and the Ark of *Remembrance*.

The Ark was constructed according to a very specific instruction given by the Lord Himself, and it was carried at the head of the Israeli army to battle. The Ark's aweome power was feared by both the Israelites and their enemies. Once, however, the Ark was captured by the enemy and, after some curious encounters, it was eventually returned to the Israeli camp. King David welcomed the Ark back to his camp with a great feast of sacrifice and music, pomp and circumstance. The Bible tells us that the king himself danced before the Ark with all his might in near nakedness, so much so that his wife Michel "despised him (for his un-kingly behavior before his servants). Afterward, King David housed the Ark in a special tabernacle (tent) that he had erected. Finally, David's son King Solomon built the most glorious Temple the likes of which the world had never seen, and housed the Seat of the Lord in the Holy of Holies inside the Temple where the Ark was to repose forever.

Why was the Ark so important? It was really not the Ark itself, essentially a wooden box but with covering of gold plates inside and out, and with golden cherubim atop the lid of solid gold. Rather, it was the *contents* in the Ark. And I am sure your learned ministers could tell you what was placed inside the Ark of the Lord. To save you time and trouble (and a possible little embarrassment to your minister), I will tell you that there were three *sacred* articles that were put inside the holy receptacle:

The most important article was a pair of stone tablets on which were inscribed the *Decalogue*, the ten words or the "Ten Commandments." (Actually this pair of stone tablets was the third pair; Moses had smashed the first pair in rage when he saw how the Israelites committed an abominable sin while he was up on Mount Horeb—also called Mount Sinai—communicating with God. With permission from Aaron who also was a brother of Moses' and a priest, the rowdy people had created a golden calf, just like one of the Egyptian gods, and worshipped it. Therefore, the Lord ordered Moses to write the law on the *second* pair. Still later and after Moses died, Joshua, the new leader of the Israelites, wrote the law on the third pair of tablets.) These stone tablets with God's written laws, were the *Commandments* that the Lord had specifically ordered His chosen people to obey for all generations.

The second item was a pot of *manna*. In case you have no idea what *manna* was, it's perfectly understandable, since even the Israelites didn't know what it was and, hence, called it *manna* (meaning "*what is it?*"). It is one of the favorite stories told and retold in Sunday school classes how the Lord had made "bread from heaven" fall on the ground early in the morning to feed the hungry multitude when there wasn't enough foodstuff to be found in the desert. Scientists have been able to assert that *manna* was a kind of plant secretion that hardens to become like small cereal or *coriander seeds*, with sweet flavor. Even today, people living in the same desert regions still refer to this organic substance as "the bread of heaven." However, to the hungry and desperate Israelites wandering in the desert, this was such a miracle of how the Lord had fed them—besides *manna*, God had also provided them with birds from the sky and fresh waters gushing out of the rock—that the Lord had commanded that a portion of *manna* be collected and put in a jar, to be kept inside the Ark to serve as *remembrance* of God's mercy for all future generations.

The third item was a rod, essentially a wooden cane, carried by Aaron. Many miracles were performed (by Moses) with this rod, and the Lord commanded that this rod of Aaron that had miraculously *budded*, also be kept in the Ark. This rod from which branches had sprouted had come to symbolize the *menorah*, the "tree of life" and subsequently became the familiar *seven-branched candle stand* that is found in every Jewish synagogue today.

With the greatest of festive jubilation the people of Israel had ever seen before or hence, King Solomon dedicated the Temple and the Ark was brought up to the Temple to be permanently reposed. However, a most incredible and puzzling thing had happened. It was discovered that, when the Ark was finally placed in the Temple (and, we may assume, when King Solomon and the priests opened the Ark), it was discovered that "*there was nothing [else] in the Ark except the two tablets of stone*"! (*cf.* First Kings 8:9). Apparently, someone had removed the two other articles, the *rod* that budded, and the *urn* that contained an amount of foodstuff (*manna*).

Subsequent to Solomon's death and a few decades later, the nation of Israel was in total disarray, divided into the North (Israel) and the South (Judah). Eventually the whole Hebrew nation was conquered by the Babylonians (sixth century, B.C.E.), the Temple was destroyed, its contents carried away, and the people taken into captivity. As the prophet lamented, "By the river of Babylon," the people wept, forsaken by the Lord. Meanwhile, the Ark vanished forever, never to be found.

In the depth of the sacred altar building of the Ise Shrine in Japan is a good-size wooden box and, according to the tradition, the sacred receptacle contains three "divine relics." The wooden chest is known by the name of *MiFune Shiro*, its literal meaning is the "*Replica of the Divine Boat*" (here, it is to be noted that "boat" is also "ark"). There are, howeveer, some puzzling mystiques about this sacred chest and its contents.

First, while the tradition holds that *MiFune Shiro* contains *san-po* (three treasures), various historical chronicles, including *Nihon Shoki*, *Kojiki*, and *Kyuji Honki* (Book Five), as well as one of the most important and incredibly detailed historical books from the early feudal era, the *Heiki Monogatari* (*The Tales of* [the *House of*] *Hei*, or the *Tahira* clans), all make reference to *only two* articles of sacred relics: the *kan-gami* (mirror); and the *tsurugi* (sword).

Second, the description of the mirror is not at all like the bronze mirrors unearthed from various archaeological excavations throughout the Eurasian continent. Rather, the item is often depicted as if it is a box, frail from incredible age and in danger of falling apart, thus requiring layers upon layers of brocade wrappings. Even more curious is the fact that the item is described as having a lid and, when opened, would emit a puff of white powder which caused irritation to people standing nearby. One plausible explanation for this contradiction betweeen the item and its name is that the *kangami* (mirror) is another case of *ateji*, erroneous use of Chinese characters to represent the pho-netic sound of the name the article was originally called. Thus, it may be supposed that if it is a divine mirror, it would have been called *mi-kagami*, and not *kan-gami*. Hence, *kan-gami* might have been a slightly mispronounced name for what actually was meant to be a *kan-game*, meaning a "divine urn."

Third, the *tsurugi* (sword) is described—and with photo to verify the shape of the article—as a curious, *seven-branched sword*. Hence this sword is also called by the name of *shichi-shi to*—the "sword with seven branches," having a shape similar to the *menorah* figure of the candle stand of Jewish synagogues. One may even venture to say that this was a replica of the "branched rod" of Aaron that was placed inside the Ark of the Covenant. (The historical record also indicates that this sword was a gift from a Korean king to the Japanese throne. But this will entail another lengthy explanation of the proto-Japanese tribe's migra-tory journey through Korea and cultural and cultic lineage between Japan and Korea. Here, it would suffice to simply mention that Japan's mythological tales are closely entwined with the legends of Korea, that the two peoples are in fact cultural and blood kindred.)

There are at least two references in these historical chronicles that mention that two emperors had the urn opened and, surprised by the puff of white powder arising from the urn, had the lid replaced immediately. White powdery smoke? Could it be that the contents of the urn, an organic substance that had been inside the sealed container for many centuries or even a couple of millennia, had turned into toxic pollen?

If so, could it be, may we venture to speculate, that a splinter tribe of the Israelites, perhaps those who were not satisfied with the current reign (of King David who had massacred countless thousands of the kindred Semitic—but not his own Israeli—tribes), had stolen the two more easily concealed articles from the Ark of the Covenant? We may further speculate that, unwilling or unable to remain within the Israelite territory, these disenchanted splinter people had carried the treasures and escaped east- and northeastward, traveled through the vast territory of the Persian Empire, even cohabitating with the common folks living within the Persian Empire (and thus adopting the *Mythra* cult of the Persian people) but later, with the political change to a harsh and cruel reign of the Assyrians and later Romans, self-exiled from the land and continued their migratory journey toward the "rising sun."

The eastward journey, another *diaspora*, would take them through the now well-secured trade route (with the Chinese and Roman garrisons) that we now call the Silk Road. Through this trade route, they would eventually enter (the present) Afghanistan and Tibet (note: the Tibetan language is in fact quite similar to the old Japanese), and descend from a rugged and unforgiving mountainous territory to a much more hospitable northern-central plains region of China. Still continuing their self-imposed diaspora eastward, they would enter modern Korea (possibly tarrying there for decades) and eventually leave Korea behind, to cross the narrow strait of water, to arrive at the island of Japan. There, finally, they would find a land devoid of any cruel reign or military threats, to arrive at the new land of—the *second*—Canaan.

I may go on to offer a few more evidences to support this incredible and wildly speculative anthropological (hypo-)thesis. But before we rush to refute outright or to acknowledge even the slightest possibility of the scenario stated above, I hope you kind readers will share with me one particular perspective: the question of "What is East and what is West, or what is Eastern people and what is Western people," anyway. The East is sometimes the West, and the West is sometimes the East. And we ought to be honest enough to admit that we simply know far too little of anything, especially when we are too far from the historical events of the past, to say with any certainty about our past, and about the relationship of man in the tumultuous cultural crosscurrents of history.

All of us are merely passengers on tiny ships amidst the ever-shifting continents and ever-drifting and crisscrossing currents of time and space. We are all one people; we are so much alike in so many ways and so different in so many other ways all at the same time. And the tales such as mentioned here, however strange and incredible they may seem, should help to make us realize that those people whom for some reason we have been conditioned to regard with indifference, disdain or even spitefulness, may indeed turn out to be our very own kind. Then, our big Jewish friend may come to realize that the little man whom he mistook for a Japanese—and even if he happened to be a Japanese—may be his own blood kin. Then, and only then, we can truly say that we are all sisters and brothers. Then, and *only then*, we can hope that the Peaceable Kingdom, where all human beings can truly coexist harmoniously, may finally be realized on this tiny planet.

[**NOTE**: Readers may find this author's recent publication *THE REPLICA OF THE ARK OF THE COVENANT IN JAPAN: The Mystery of MiFune Shiro,* of considerable interest, as it treats this subject much more fully.]

8

Visiting China, My Ancestral Land

In July 1990, I was invited to attend the first symposium of the newly founded SOCIETY FOR RESEARCH IN AMERICAN MUSIC (SRAM), held in Jinan, Shangdong Province, some ten-hour train ride east of Beijing. Boarding the plane at Dallas-Fort Worth Airport, I felt overwhelmed by a realization that for the first time in my life I would be visiting the land of my ancestors. Born and raised in Taiwan, with Japanese as my first language until about ten years old, I had never had any firsthand knowledge of China and, in fact, had never had any feeling of kinship with its people. That was until this first visit.

Some twenty hours of flight from DFW Airport, the plane landed in Beijing. Prof. George Papastavrou (Syracuse University School of Music) and I, the only two American professors who accepted the invitation to the conference, were received warmly by a delegation of the symposium officials at the airport, and we were transported to the hotel in a *very old* VW van. The seats, with all the cushions hard-pressed flat, were less than comfortable, especially after such a long flight and the nearly one-hour ride from the airport to the hotel. But the cool and humid night air of Beijing streets felt wonderfully exciting. For I was in the land of my ancestors, the land of Confucius and Menfucius, the land which boasts one of the earliest and most advanced civilizations in the ancient world.

I rose early the next morning; jet lag was playing havoc on my body clock. For I woke up at about three o'clock in the wee predawn hours, and I was getting very impatient with the slow movement of my alarm clock. As soon as there was enough light on the street, I ventured out, alone. The street in front of *Renmin Da-Fandian* (People's Hotel) was wide, clean, and strangely quiet. I immediately noticed that there were few automobiles and, instead, hundreds of bicycles were moving—more like flowing—eerily quietly, like converter belts on both sides of the wide thoroughfare.

I started walking, not knowing where, just anxious to become a part of this city, this country, and its people whom I have come to renew—actually to foster a new—acquaintance. At the front of the hotel, I decided to turn right and continue walking in the same direction, admiring the trees and shrubs planted along the sides of the thoroughfare. There were people, municipal employees, I was sure, who were sweeping and otherwise cleaning the sidewalks. Whenever I caught the eye of one of the street sweepers, I would say "*zao*!" (good morning), and discovered that such a greeting from a total stranger caught them quite off guard. Still, I kept on repeating my Texan manner (people in Texas do say "Hi" or "Howdy" to nearly everyone they pass by on the street) as I began the venture.

After about ten minutes or so walking, the vista in front of me suddenly opened up wide, really wide. I found myself standing at one corner of a huge public square, each side framed by an impressively large building. Suddenly, I realized that the one on the side of my walk was *the* Forbidden City, and the huge square in front of it was the now world-famous Tian-An-Men Square. For, only a little over a year before, this was the epicenter of the 'democratic demonstrations' led by thousands of Chinese college students, the event that had aroused the attention of the news media worldwide. I stood there, turned around and around, looked up to the huge portrait of Chairman Mao Tzedong above the gate of the Forbidden Palace, and tried to sort out myriads of thoughts racing through my mind. Though I had no intimate knowledge of the history of China, I knew that the compound behind the impressive "heavenly" gate was the palace residence of the emperors during the Ming and Qing dynasties, from the fourteenth century to the first decade of the twentieth century.

This was the seat of the throne that epitomized the might and glory that once was China, and this very palace became also the scene of the tragedies that unfolded at the end of imperial China, by the invasion of the allied forces of the eight Western countries (including America), and by its own people. Beginning in the seventeenth century, imperial China was shaken from its very foundation. For, soon after Columbus reached the West Indies, and Magellan and his men completed the circumnavigational voyage around the world, nearly the whole of Europe literally descended on the Far East, forcing open the ports of Japan and China with firearms and canons, and with their ominous *black ships*. The once proud, secluded and invincible China was made aware of the forces and the wisdom of the "barbarian" nations that had pried open the complacent and arrogant mindset of China.

The seventeenth century marked the beginning of the end of imperial China that was established long before there was the Greek and the Babylonian empires. For over five thousand years, China—or *Zhong-Guo*, the name that connotes "The Central Kingdom"—was the most civilized country in the entire world, with advanced technologies and the "wisdom of heaven and earth" (*i.e.*, the natural and physical sciences) that far surpassed all other lands of the ancient world. China had formulated a numerical system based on the *decimal* principle of calculation as early as the second millennium B.C.E., about three thousand five hundred years before Europe finally abandoned the Roman-numeral system for mathematical tabulation and adopted the Arabic numeral system (which also was based on the decimal principle). As long as four thousand years ago, Chinese astrologers had recorded the world's earliest observed super novae, and meticulously registered all the solar and lunar eclipses.

The Chinese were the world's first discoverers of many inventions that had ushered in the "modern" age of science and technology, such as the compass (the ancient Chinese called it *zi-nan-zen*, or "south-pointing needle"), and gunpowder. They had discovered how to *untangle* the silkworm cocoon, to spin silk threads and to make silk fabrics, when people in some European regions were still using animal hides for clothing. Incredibly light, soft and *silky* delicate, silk was the most prized commodity in the world, said to value its weight in gold. The dare-devil merchants and traders ventured nature's harsh elements, impossible terrains, and perils of robbers and bandits to travel the width of the Eurasian continent to reach the land of Cathay (China), for the singular purpose of trading for silk. In the Roman Empire, silk was the symbol of a person's elevated status in society. Legend has it that this all started when Julius Caesar wore the silk garb to attend a public event in the coliseum. Amidst the incessant "oohs" and "ahs" of all the people at the coliseum, the Romans was struck by the realization that their emperor had demonstrated his unimaginable wealth and power by the single gown entirely made of silk.

The Chinese were also the inventor of the "moveable" printing press around the tenth century. However, it took nearly half a millennium for Europe to finally adopt the invention. The cause of the delay in adopting this most important invention of civilization—the propagation of knowledge through printed books—was rather silly, rooted in cultural and cultic belief. Arabs and Middle-Eastern merchants had been trading with China, and had brought Chinese merchandise and useful tools of invention to the West for many centuries. But they refused to adopt the printing press technology. The reason was that the Chinese used the brush to first write the calligraphy on a wooden block, in reversed image, then carved out the letters to make the master block for mass printing. But, alas, the brush was made of *pig's bristle*, and no self-respecting Muslims would have anything to do with pigs or pig parts, including the hair.

China was known throughout the civilized world as the land of unimaginable wealth, superb knowledge, and formidable military might. And all the neighboring countries, from the Middle and Near East to the southeastern regions of Asia brought tributes to the imperial courts of China, in exchange for trade favoritism and military protection. In return, China had generously provided the requested needs, and shared its knowledge and sent political emissaries and military garrisons. It might be of interest to note that many European dishes have their origin in China: German *sauerkraut* was created in China, during the long years of constructing the Great Walls. When thousands of laborers began to become ill and even died (from lack of vegetable in their diet and short on vitamin C), some clever cook discovered that *cabbage boiled in brine* (salt water) would preserve the vegetable almost indefinitely and thus could be transported far and preserved as long as necessary. This concoction was subsequently adopted by the Turks and, from there, it reached Europe. Italian spaghetti was the Chinese *mien* (noodle), and pizza was Chinese *dabin* (large and flat cake). Even the sauce that goes on pizza came from China. The sause is essentially fruit (tomato) juice that the Chinese call *guo-zhi* or, in southern dialect, *ga-zhap* and it eventually became *ca-tsap*. Today, we see with a little discomfort how China still exports its product to the whole world, to the extent that it is virtually impossible to imagine a normal household without the myriad of merchandise items that are all marked "MADE IN CHINA."

Soon after the Forbidden City in Beijing was constructed, the court of the Ming Dynasty in the early fifteenth century undertook what is arguably the greatest naval expedition the world had ever seen. A huge armada consisting of several hundred ships, the large ones capable of holding hundreds of people on board, all built to withstand the long voyage in the open sea lasting several months, sailed down the full length of the coast of southeast Asia, and navigated westward to arrive at the Arabian and African coasts. The expedition was repeated several times in the ensuing years and, on one of the last expeditions, one part of the naval fleet went up northward, and sailed as far northeast as the northern coasts of the North American continent. A colony of Chinese was established there, long before Columbus and his men had reached the West Indies on three rather primitive ships.

Indeed, China's historical past was glorious beyond description. I visited the *Tian-An Men* Square (the "Gate of Heavenly Peace") and the "Purple" Forbidden Palace (now a national museum; the color purple was symbolic of the imperial throne). A few days later, I visited an aged building and walked the hallways where Confucius had taught in *peripatetic* fashion. I also visited the site of Confucius' grave, climbed the Great Walls, and walked the banks of the Huang River, the very cradle of China's civilization. And I could not help feeling proud, perhaps for the first time in my life, that I am a child of this land. For this land and its people have sustained the longest civilization in the world, the longest surviving and living language in the world, and I can still read and speak the same language that the ancient Chinese sages wrote and spoke—the great philosophers Confucius and Menfucius, who had lived and taught some five centuries before Christ, as well as the beautiful verses of the immortal poets Li Bai and Du Fu.

It may appear incongruous to many readers that, with all this talk about China's glorious past, its superb achievements in virtually every field of science and, if indeed China had made such a remarkable contribution to the world, what had happened that had caused China to fall so far behind in virtually everything, proving itself so tragically inept in defending itself against the invading forces of the Western countries during the eighteenth and nineteenth centuries, and even the first half of the twentieth?

The answer, it goes without saying, is a much more complex one than this short article or even this series of "The East is East, and The West is West" articles could ever sufficiently provide. However, though fully aware of the very likelihood of being accused of over-simplification, gross generalization, or even callous oversight of many relevant historical facts, I would nevertheless like to offer my own version of an explanation.

The problem that had affected the internal decay and caused the eventual downfall of Imperial China had to do with the government bureaucracy and religious polity, the two systems that were controlled by the self-appointed spokesmen for the people and the spokesmen for gods. This may sound rather "contemporary" and a fashionable thing to do, to blame whatever woes in the world on the errors of ways of the government and the church. This is, actually, rather understandable and to be expected, as government and church polities are the two institutions where the worst of human nature—greed for wealth and power, and arrogance of self-righteousness—finds fertile soil. It is here that history is repeated over and over, in the East as well as in the West. Personages, places, and times may differ, but the essence of the stories themselves rings familiar. And one of my most favorite of all historical anecdotes about China's early contacts with the West, the "national experience" which brought to light what had been ailing China from within, has to do with the clock, the kind that would go tick-tock and sound ding-dong on the hour and half an hour.

Soon after the European black ships charted the navigational routes along the coasts of the Far Eastern countries, traders and missionaries—both came with the sanction and blessings of the Mother Church—forced open a few ports of call on the western shores of the Pacific Ocean. In Japan, it was Nagasaki and Yokohama and, in China, it was Macao and Hong Kong a century or so later. From the late sixteenth century, trade fairs were held in Macao, and these fairs provided the European traders and missionaries the best of opportunities to not only trade commodities of European fancies but also to acquire books and works of art. For the entire Europe suddenly recalled the travelogue of Marco Polo describing the unimaginable wealth and superior wisdom of Cathay (China). The Vatican was particularly excited by the prospect, a recognition of the new vast golden field ripe for harvest, and missionaries from various orders—Augustinian, Franciscan, etc. and, later, the Jesuits—converged on these eastern shores.

Chinese books were highly prized by the early missionaries to China, as most of these men of cloth were scholars in their own right. In particular, members of the Society of Jesus, more commonly known as Jesuits, who were sent to Asia were highly educated, equipped with the newest scientific and mathematical knowledge taught in the strenuous curriculum of the newly founded Roman College in the Vatican City. This was deemed important, as reports sent by the early missionaries back to the Vatican had made the Church aware of the fact that Asians were highly intelligent and civilized (as compared to the people on other early missionary frontiers such as South and North America), where nothing less than the best of Western scholarship would be able to persuade and proselytize the populace and bring them to the fold of the Mother Church. Besides, this was the land of silk and porcelain, of rare and prized spices, and numerous other rare commodities that the European high societies craved after.

Among the early scholar-missionaries was a young Jesuit priest named Matteo Ricci. He arrived at Macao in 1582, sent there because his supervisor had recognized his intense missionary zeal and unusual intellectual and linguistic capacity. Before being summoned to Macao, he was sent to India for a few years, where he had observed how harshly the natives were treated by the missionaries who performed their evangelical duties as if in military camp, with whips, chains and penal codes. Through this experience, Ricci had fathomed an entirely different mindset regarding his missionary task and, immediately after arriving in Macao, he undertook an earnest study not only to speak but also to write Chinese proficiently.

This was a formidable task (ask any missionary to China) but, after two years in Macao, he succeeded in obtaining permission from a Chinese (regional) government to cross the narrow bay from Macao to enter the China mainland. First, he was granted a small residence in a small town near (about an hour's car ride from) Guangdong. There, he used his scientific knowledge—mathematics, geometry, astrology, and cartography in particular—to his advantage in attracting, raising the curiosity of, and befriending the local intelligentsia (the Confucian scholars) and government officials. Soon he was able to build a small mission house, built in traditional Chinese style architecture. Still, he was not content with these small successes. For Ricci had his eyes set on Beijing, on *Jing-gong* or *Zhi Jing-gong*, the "Purple Forbidden Palace" (purple was the color of the imperial household), the residence of the emperor known as the "forbidden" palace. For Ricci had the (Apostle) Paul's evangelical zeal, to bring the Gospel to the imperial court. Ricci envisioned that, like the Apostle Paul who had brought the knowledge of Christianity to the Caesar's court (even if not successful in making any converts), he too will bring the Gospel to the court of the Ming emperor.

The reason the emperor's residence was referred to as the "forbidden" palace was because no man (male) was allowed to remain within the huge palace compound after sunset, not even the high officials of the court, or the emperor's own relatives regardless of their status. For it was the residence of the emperor alone and, of course, his "harem" of wives and consorts of various ranks, all told to number several hundred to a couple of thousand. (Of course, we know that this was common in ancient times, East and West. For Christians, we may be reminded that King David had many, many wives, including the wives of the former king Saul. King Solomon, being the wealthiest and his court the mightiest, had gathered many—about a thousand—wives from all regions, of all complexions, and he loved them to the extent that he built temples for worship of his wives' exotic gods.) And, in a palace where countless wives and consorts (a polite word for concubines) lived and complained day and (especially) night of not getting enough attention from the emperor, any male remaining within such an environment after dark would be like letting loose a fox in a chicken coop.

To say that no man (male) was allowed within the palace compound was not exactly accurate. In reality, there were a large number—a few thousand—of men of special class who were allowed to remain within the *forbidden city* after dark. They were the eunuchs. In case you are not familiar with the particular *pre*-requisite for becoming an eunuch, the following may "enlighten" you on this peculiar practice in the ancient world, in the East and the West. First, to become an eunuch, a man must be relatively young and healthy in order to undergo a very special physical "alteration" called *castration*. The castration for eunuchs in China was a *complete* procedure, as compared to the Western procedure—especially the Italian *castrati* kind—that was only *par-*

tial. The rest of the requisites for becoming an eunuch may not need explanation since they are, well, rather ordinary by comparison. Thus enlightened (or *lightened*), these *men* were now deemed qualified to remain in the imperial residence, since they have been certified to be *un-threatening*. And day and night, these eunuchs lived in relative comfort with only one specific appointed duty—to serve and minister the emperor, to ensure that the emperor's needs, great and small, were completely met.

When the sun sets in the western sky and the palace compound is all quiet, the eunuchs have yet another specific task to perform. It should be mentioned that the original meaning of the word *eunuch* (of Greek origin) is "the one who *watches* [the emperor's] *bed chamber.*" For, you see, while the emperor had only one empress, he also had several wives all neatly classified into various ranks (about twelve, a nice auspicious number), as well as even a far greater number of consorts, all vying for the attention and affection of the son of heaven. This would create a problem in establishing any sort of orderly routine for scheduling these wives and consorts a private time with the emperor, a logistical problem that is literally a *night*mare for those watchers of the bedchamber.

Ah, the wisdom of man and the belief in his ability to comprehend the wisdom of heaven. The wise ancient China had in fact established a schedule of the affairs of the emperor's chamber as early as the Zhou dynasty. In *Li Ji*, the *Manual of Rites*, details of the schedule of the affairs of chamber were well established, laying out the precise schema on how many wives and how many consorts were to enter the emperor's bed chamber on which of the nights of the lunar months, all according to proper numerology. This scheme was laid out in meticulous detail so that the empress would have one unencumbered—that is, un-competing—night alone with the emperor, on the night of the full moon, when it was believed that the forces of *yin* and *yang* would be in perfect alignment, thus ensuring the most auspicious conception of the emperor's heir.

In the palace compound, just outside the emperor's bedchamber, was a clock tower. Why would the Chinese place the clock tower in the inner courtyard of the imperial palace, instead of in the town center and atop the town hall, as in many old and more recent European cities, for example? Because it was a politically and religiously astute thing to do, since the survival of the empire depends on the timing of performance of administrative affairs in strict and accurate accordance with the timing of the movement of the spirit of nature, and that can only be achieved by having an accurate calendar and accurate clock. You see, one of the most sacred of all the duties of an emperor was to announce the calendrical events, such as the day of the new moon, the vernal and autumnal equinoxes and summer and winter solstices.

This was true in all ancient cultures, East and West, since the survival of an agrarian society depended critically on an accurate knowledge of seasonal changes. Even in nomadic society, the "feast of the new moon" was an all-important ritual occasion, and the Old Testament gives many accounts of the early Israelites' observance of the new-moon festival, with the sounding of a *shofar* (ram's horn), priestly prayers and musical performances. And since the emperors or kings were supposed to have been appointed and anointed by the heaven, he should have the ability to accurately announce changes in celestial and terrestrial phenomena. An accurate calendar and an accurate clock would be indispensable to the emperor in performing such a heavenly-appointed task.

Therefore, as early as the eleventh century, a gigantic time-piece—actually an astronomical machine, complete with moving human figures striking the gigantic bells to sound the hours of the day and night—was invented in China, a machine that was also capable of showing the relative positions of the sun, the moon, and the known planets. This marvelously crafted and highly sophisticated astronomical time machine, or clock, some thirty feet high, was presented to the throne, and was placed in the inner courtyard of the imperial palace.

There was another reason for the clock tower to be placed so near the bed chamber of the emperor: to allow the eunuchs to better observe the time of the day and night in keeping with the ritual (lunar) calendar, and to ensure the most accurate time when the emperor and the empress should conduct the affairs of the chamber, at the precise and most auspicious moment when the cosmic forces are in perfect alignment. Indeed, there was nothing more important in imperial China to ensure the continuity of the blood lineage of the son of heaven, and all wisdom of mathematics, astrology and calendar were employed to ensure the un-interrupted continuity of the imperial lineage.

It was for this reason, too, that in ancient China, anyone, whether a commoner or a government official, found in possession of a calendar, clock or chart of movement of celestial bodies, was accused of treason of undermining the stability of the imperial house. And thus convicted—these instruments were the iron proof of the crime—the guilty were summarily put to death by beheading, or worse (*e.g.*, separation of limbs by four or five horses galloping off in all directions).

As was mentioned, the young Jesuit priest Matteo Ricci arrived in Macao in 1582 and was eventually admitted within China's borders to establish a mission house in Guangdong. With his eyes and heart set on the Forbidden Palace, he wrote a letter of petition to the emperor, submitting that he had come from far beyond the oceans, in admiration of the glory of the empire and virtuous deeds of the emperor anointed by heaven, that he longed for an audience with the son of heaven and, if so granted, wanted to present to the throne gifts from beyond the "far western seas." (I have read a reprint of Ricci's letter and it was most eloquent and exceedingly refined.) Ricci even described the gift items, among them a harpsichord, and two clocks—the kind that not only would show the hours and minutes of the day but also chime on the hour. Little did Ricci know at the time of his writing the letter that it was his mention of the clocks that would not only open the door of the Forbidden Palace to him but would also save his and his companion's life from execution by beheading. [To be continued on the next episode.]

9

Clocks, Eunuchs, and the Jesuits

Even before receiving any reply from the Palace, Ricci and his companion set out for Beijing. The journey from Guangdong to Beijing, today a mere two-hour-plus flight, proved to be difficult and hazardous and, altogether, it took more than two years to complete. The journey was a dangerous one, made more so due to the suspicion on the part of local Chinese people and officials not wholly willing to lend assistance, and by the elements which caused two shipwrecks. *En route*, they were also imprisoned: the Japanese and Portuguese pirates were ravaging the coastal routes, and all foreigners were regarded as suspect.

Once they were imprisoned for suspicion of practicing human sacrifice, because the Chinese solders regarded *crucifix* in the priest's possessions as the emblem of human sacrifice. And they thought that they would surely face a worst fate. But, suddenly, they were not only let go from the prison cells, but were escorted by official guards all the way to the Forbidden Palace. Why? Because one day the youthful emperor had remembered reading the letter from a foreign priest in which it was mentioned that *clocks that chime on the hour* would be presented to the throne. The emperor was terribly fascinated by the news of a self-chiming clock, and he ordered an investigation on the priest's whereabouts, and to bring him and the clock to the Palace.

In January 1601, Matteo Ricci and his companion finally arrived in Beijing, and were escorted to the Palace, along with their gifts to the throne. The gift items included pictures of the Virgin Mary and Infant Christ, a rhinoceros 'horn' (which the Chinese thought was the horn of a mythological unicorn), a small harpsichord, a prism, a copy of the Bible and, of course, the clocks. The smaller one was a table clock, and the tall one was the floor model. The emperor was not present at the presentation of the gifts, however. For the son of heaven could not be seen by commoners, let alone the nameless barbarians from an alien land. Still, the honored and deeply grateful priests made the clocks chime, to the surprise and delight of the eunuchs and the court officials. Thereafter, the priests were dismissed from the court and were retired to a small guesthouse outside the Palace grounds (but still within the Forbidden City).

A few days later, the worried eunuchs came rushing to summon Ricci and his companion back to the Palace; one of the clocks had failed to chime, and the emperor was not *amused!* The emperor had ordered the eunuchs to repair the "damaged" clock immediately but, poor eunuchs, they were totally and hopelessly ignorant about the Western contraption. Worse, the emperor was known for his short temper, and would not hesitate to order a man's head chopped off for even a minor offense. The eunuchs had already lost one *end* of their body to enter the service of the emperor, and now they feared that failure to repair the emperor's new toy may well cost them another part on the other end of their body—I mean, their heads.

The Jesuits gladly obliged and quickly fixed the damage. Actually the clock did not chime because the eunuchs did not wind the springs and lift the weight. Still, the eunuchs were greatly comforted that the clocks could chime again. The deeply grateful eunuchs, who only a little while ago were adamant in not admitting Ricci and his companion to the palace, advising the throne that the presence of the barbarians would surely contaminate the sanctity and purity of the throne, now realized that they owed their life's debt to these same aliens. The delighted emperor also ordered that Ricci and his companion were authorized to enter the palace freely, without any written permission. Thereafter, the emperor had a clock tower specifically designed and built in the inner courtyard to house the tall clock, but placed the small clock in his bed chamber, and appointed an eunuch to wind the clock daily without fail.

With the trust of the eunuchs and a tacit approval of the throne safely tucked in his pocket (just an expression; I don't know if priests' garbs came with pockets), Ricci set out to convert China. His tactic was an altogether unique, "accommodating" approach. Unlike his Jesuit brethren sent to India and North and South America who treated the natives as uncivilized heathens and sub-human, Ricci recognized the high level of civilization and scientific knowledge that the Chinese had already attained and, thus, he did his best to win the Chinese over to the side of Christendom by way of intellectual persuasion. First, Ricci began to dress like Confucian literati, and adopted a Chinese name Li Madou. He wrote religious and ethical pamphlets in Chinese. His knowledge of not only the Chinese spoken language but also Chinese classic literature (such as the writing of Confucius and Menfucius) was so proficient and extensive that he was able to carry on dialogue with court officials and Confucian literati. Then Ricci began to focus on the areas of scientific knowledge that he knew the Chinese to be lagging behind their European counterpart. They were geometry, astrology (astronomy) and cartography, particularly the last two.

Actually, the Chinese had already attained a high level of scientific knowledge in both astronomy and cartography (map making), and all such superior knowledge was meticulously registered in myriads of

treatises, safely deposited and tucked away deep inside the huge imperial archives. The world's first and, even today, the greatest encyclope-
dic work, running into thousands of volumes, was produced even
before Ricci arrived in China.

But that, precisely, was also where the problem lay: the greatest
deposits of human knowledge and accomplishment were in the court
or the government archives, unavailable to the common people, left
unexamined and, eventually, forgotten. The eunuchs, whose interests
were always in self-serving and self-preserving, became the guardian of
the imperial archives and even the availability of the emperor for advice
and recommendation of court officials. Even the Bureau of Rites that
officiated all the rituals of the court was controlled by those scheming
and personal gain-driven eunuchs. And for self-aggrandizing and
patronizing the emperor and boosting the arrogance of the collective
psyche, the only kind of map eunuchs would allow in the court was
one that would show the imperial court drawn large in the center, with
the border of China occupying the greater part of the space, showing
that China was indeed the "Central Kingdom."

When an astrolabe—an astronomical instrument that showed the
position of the sun, the planets and the moon relative to the
earth—was moved from the old capital to Beijing when the Forbidden
City was constructed, the eunuchs did not even bother to inquire, even
if they knew they did not have sufficient knowledge, to realign the
instrument. As a result, the predictions of solar and lunar eclipses and
prognostications of the arrival of summer and winter solstices and vernal and autumnal equinoxes, issued by the Bureau of Rites, were more
than often wrong.

Since the ancient Chinese believed that the throne was divinely
anointed, where the emperor would sit as the son of heaven, the ability
of the Bureau of Rites to accurately predict and prognosticate the sea-

sonal changes and the movements of celestial bodies were the sign of god's approval of the dynasty's mandate to rule the land. But when the prognostications went awry, sometimes off by a few hours to even a few days, the Bureau would announce that this was an ominous sign from heaven, to forewarn the people of some impending disaster. "Repent, and all shall be well" was the message to the populace. Such was the state of the Chinese imperial court's bureaucratic nonsense and numerological hocus pocus, created largely by the ranks of eunuchs (counting to over four thousand by the end of China's dynastic reign in the first decade of the twentieth century) that reached a level of chaos of national proportion when Ricci arrived in the Forbidden Palace.

Ricci lived in China for nearly three decades, the last of which within the imperial city. During the last nine years of his life there, he had met literally thousands of literati and scholar-officials, to the extent that he sometimes had to forego his meals. In 1610, Ricci died in his residence in Beijing, due mainly to sheer exhaustion from giving himself so unreservedly to the people to whom he had come to minister. Upon hearing of his death, the emperor allocated a plot of land for Ricci's burial; he was buried with the full honor of a person of highest official distinction in the imperial domain.

Although Ricci did not succeed in bringing the imperial household to the Christian faith, he had indeed sowed the seed that is still bearing fruition today, even after four centuries. Among his few converts were three prominent scholar officials of the court. One of them even became the director of the Bureau of Rites, and implemented the solar calendar to correct the ritual calendar of the court so distorted and disaligned by the eunuchs. Another one translated *Geometria* (written by Eucles of ancient Greece) into Chinese, and all three contributed greatly to the propagation of Christianity in China. Even today, some

Chinese clock merchants in the southern coastal provinces still revered Ricci as a *boddhishattva* (a demigod in Buddhism faith). (This is similar to the Catholic faithful praying through Virgin Mary or one of the saints, believing that their prayers to these once-human figures would have a better chance to be heard than propitiating directly to the Divine Head.)

In the summer of 1996, my wife and I were granted a rare privilege of an escorted visit—no less than a personal pilgrimage—to the memorial ground of Ricci where he and some dozen of his fellow Jesuit missionary priests also have their final resting place. The memorial is inside a communist-party political college, inaccessible to the common populace. The impressive memorial plaque—the head stone—for Ricci, well over sixteen feet high, had inscriptions in two languages, Latin and Chinese, still clearly legible even after four centuries. Standing by Ricci's memorial plaque, one can be overwhelmed by the realization that here rests the man who had done so much for the betterment of the fellow citizens of his adopted country, who so readily became a gentile or, in this case, one of the Chinese, in order to win them to Christ. He even saw the common spiritual threads between the Christian doctrine and Chinese (Confucian) concepts of man and gods, and adopted Chinese terms from their ancient religious writings to refer to the Christian God and Christ. (Incidentally, it was Ricci who also gave us the name *Confucius* for *Kong Fu-zi*.) Indeed, he was the first true bridge between the East and the West in things religious, spiritual, scientific and cultural. In the life and death of Matteo Ricci, there was no East or West.

After Ricci's death, the Vatican sent another group of Jesuit priests to China. Among them was Adam Schall von Bell, a German Jesuit who was a truly learned man, versed in the most current mathematical and astronomical knowledge. Schall von Bell even brought telescopes to China, originally a kind of spying glass that Galileo made improvements on and pointed it skyward and, with it, verified the heliocentric theory proposed earlier by Nicholai Copernicus. Unlike Copernicus, however, Galileo was able to escape the fate of burning at the stake, perhaps only because he had some friends in high places, including a personal acquaintance with the Pope, and thus was only on imposed house arrest. It is of considerable irony that, while the whole of Europe was embroiled in the Galilean controversy and the whole scientific community was under close scrutiny of the Inquisition, this group of Jesuit priests had brought with them the Galilean telescopes, and Chinese court astrologers studied Galilean theory of cosmology and put the telescope to good use.

One of the most remarkable events was when the imperial Bureau of Rites issued a prognostication of an impending solar eclipse, to occur on the morning of June 21, 1629, at 10:30, that would last for two hours. Schall von Bell's calculation showed otherwise, and he countered that the eclipse would occur at 11:30 instead, and would last a mere two minutes. And when Schall von Bell's prediction was proven more accurate than that of the revered imperial Bureau of Rites, even the shrewd—and often deceitful—eunuch officers had to concede and admit their errors or even their lack of adequate knowledge, for the emperor and his entire imperial retinue were also present and witnessed the "contest." The prompt repentance of these eunuchs was the only way left for them to save their necks. (This scene reminds me of the contest between Elijah the prophet of Yahweh and the priests of Baal as told in the Bible, though perhaps not as dramatic. Priests of Baal lost their heads, while the Chinese eunuchs only lost face.)

Soon after this event, the old leadership of the Bureau of Rites was dismissed, and Zu Goangqim, an official of the Bureau and one of the converts and close friends of Ricci, was appointed to the directorship of the Bureau. Eventually, Schall von Bell succeeded Xu to the Bureau's directorship, marking the first—perhaps the only—time in the entire history of China when a foreigner was appointed to the most revered position in an imperial agency.

Sadly, however, the ever cunning and scheming eunuchs did not let their defeat rest and, instead, plotted revenge. They concocted an accusation of "spying for the West" against Schall von Bell. He was terribly ill and was unable to defend himself, and was convicted of the crime and sentenced to death. The execution was never carried out, however. An earthquake occurred on the day of his execution, convincing the throne that heaven was angry, and a fire broke out in the inner court on the day of the second execution, and the empress feared that, again, god was intervening.

Adam Schall von Bell died in Beijing in 1644, while still under house arrest. His large portrait hangs high on the left wall just inside the entrance to the Library (the Reading Room) of Ricci Institute, of The University of San Francisco.

Meanwhile, the Chinese were making noticeable advancement in geometry, cartography, and astronomy in particular, and were able to not only duplicate the Galilean telescope but also made improvement on the instrument. During all this experience in the first-ever true East-West encounter, both the political and religious emissaries from the West began to learn quickly what gifts would most please the Chinese officials: clocks. From then on, clocks were regarded as the choicest item for bribing (and how well we know the politicians are easily swayed by a little bribing, nowadays with the use of a corporate jet, or a vacation at an exotic resort). Hence, literally thousands of European clocks of all sizes and ornate shapes, with all the artistic intricacy and mechanical ingenuity, were presented to marvel and delight the imperial court and court officials. Today, one can still visit the Palace

Museum, one in Taipei, Taiwan (with a far richer holding of China's national treasures from remote antiquity), and the other in Beijing, just off the Tian-An-Men Square, and see in wonderment those countless magnificently crafted and intricately ornate timepieces from the early seventeenth- to the eighteenth-century Europe, all superbly preserved, with many still in good working condition.

It is profoundly amusing to think that those little—and some not so little—clocks (the largest I have seen was in Beijing's Palace Museum, almost the size of a Volkswagen) had played such a crucial role in the early stages of East-West contact. These timepieces that were intended only to tell time and perhaps also to play to the fancy of European aristocrats had proven themselves more powerful than guns and cannons in helping to open the gates of the Forbidden Palace to the early Jesuits and, in turn, to open the mind's eye of China. The near magical power of these clocks was even extended to regulate the affairs of the bedchamber of Chinese emperors, and is still felt no less powerfully over man's daily affairs, night and day, East and West.

10

The Sacred and the Profane, and Word of God and Word of Man

Some of my earliest childhood memories are those of my parents in the church; my minister father standing at the pulpit preaching, and my mother sitting at a small *Yamaha* pump organ playing when my father also led the singing of a very small congregation, perhaps no more than twenty or thirty people. We, my sisters and I, were also told Bible stories, although I do not recall reading the Bible in my primary school years, and was never taught to memorize any Bible verses. During my junior high years in Hualien (my father was no longer the resident minister of a church there), I continued to attend Sunday school and Bible study classes but, there, too, the only Bible reading was on a few selected verses for the lesson. It was not until the summer before my senior year that I made the first of my feeble attempts at reading the Bible in any systematic way. The attempt was motivated by Phillip, a cousin of mine who was in the same high school class (but not in the same home room) and who later went on to become a minister. That summer, he devoted himself to reading the entire Bible, every word and every verse, from Genesis to Revelation.

I said that it was my first "feeble attempt," because, to this day, I still have not read through the entire Bible. For one thing, those long chapters on confusing genealogy (the X begat Y, and Y begat Z, *et cetra, et cetra*), or on those strange Mosaic laws and bylaws that were narrated repetitiously in different passages, held very little relevance for me, and I simply have not had the will or the patience to follow what my much more devout cousin had done some half a century ago. During my seminary and graduate school years I did take a few theology courses, among them the class on the BOOK OF ISAIAH that was truly wonderful (I believe the professor made a difference). But I dropped out of SYSTEMATIC THEOLOGY class after only two weeks of class (the professor also made the difference).

Even today, I would follow the occasional urge to reread the Bible passages of historical account, and at times would even refer to concordances and Bible commentaries (including the less *kosher* books such as Isaac Asimov's two books on the Bible) to help clarify some details. The Bible is in many ways a fascinating candid book where some otherwise 'unspeakable affairs' between man and woman are laid bare for all to read.

There apparently were no social or moral issues raised before the Bible was translated into *vernacular* languages, because Latin was believed to be the only sanctified language, and the common people were forbidden to read the holy writ. Whatever the church and the priests said, it was regarded as the inerrant word of God. Then, the Bible began to be translated into the language of the commoners, first the *Geneva Bible* in the sixteenth century and then the *King James* version in the early seventeenth. Although still regarded as a forbidden act, the common people began to read and found certain passages troubling, and began to raise social and moral issues. In fact there actually was a self-claimed moralist in Boston nearly a century ago tried to get a court injunction against the Gideon Society in placing bibles in hotels, on the grounds that the Bible contains many "obscene and immoral" stories.

Since my high school days, I have had some lingering questions about certain narratives in the bible, and I would occasionally pose them to my father for answers. He was always receptive, open-minded, and never regarded my questions as improper, imprudent or impertinent. When he had no immediate answer, he would always say "You will need to find the answer for yourself. But you must remember that the Bible is a book of faith, and faith is a very personal thing, and only your own mind and heart can lead you to the answer you look for."

In my more innocent years back in Taiwan, I used to believe that all Christians were beholden to not only the same doctrinal creeds but also the same ethical and moral principles and behavioral underpinnings. For example, cursing and gambling are "no-nos" and smoking and drinking are unbecoming of children of God. Then—I remember well how surprised I was—one day, shortly after World War II, I saw at the train station in Keelung (a port city near Taipei), two American Catholic priests both with cigarettes in their hands. After coming to the United States, I also discovered that denominations have their own selective set of moral-ethical dos and donts. For example, the Baptists smoke but don't drink; the Methodists drink but don't smoke; and Catholics and Presbyterians both drink and smoke, or something to that effect. And, of course, it is common knowledge that while all Christians eat pork, Jews and Muslims regard it as unclean and as an abomination. And it is an irony of man's perception that, because of such beliefs, Europe had let itself lag about five centuries behind China in book printing. Europe did not have to wait until the mid-fifteenth century to produce the first mass-produced book, the Guttenberg Bible. For the traders from the Middle East, who ventured the perils on the Silk Roads and introduced so many things from China to the West for countless centuries, steadfastly refused to introduce the Chinese technique of a printing press only because the Chinese used the *pig-bristle brush* to create the master plate.

Such was the greater irony of religion that too often equated man's daily deeds and social etiquette with piety of spirit. In the name of God, man had created numerous ways to assess the degree of his spiritual devotion. And when man equates his own social customs and cultural traditions as divinely appointed, he monopolizes God, making God in man's own image. God became one of his, and not of the others. Once, when I was at a fundamental Christian university in the South, I asked my theology-major roommates about a certain passage in the Bible that had puzzled me for some time, and I was virtually branded as literal and heretical. In that self-appointed "Westpoint of the Christian faith," you could argue just about anything; football, weather, even politics. But when it regards God or the Bible, there was absolutely no room for free thinking, let alone questioning aloud.

The question I asked was about how the Lord blessed King David and, in victory, delivered not only the palaces, gold and silver into his hands, but also the "wives of [King Saul] into [King David's] bosom" (II Samuel 12:7, *ff*). (Such stories abound in the book of Genesis. Try reading Chapter 38, about the story of Tamar and Judah, her father in-law, and see if you could remain indifferent to biblical perspective of ethical propriety.) My question went something like this (I am rephrasing it much better than my broken English was a few decades ago):

> "Do you think God really *gave* King Saul's wives (plural) to King David as a reward, or Nathan (the prophet) was attaching a religious perspective to the social custom of the time? I know that such custom was also practiced in China and many ancient societies, that a victorious king would inherit all the wives of the defeated king as a part of the spoils of war. But, if that was indeed God's

will, then do you think God has changed his opinion about *polygamy* and *monogamy*?"

It was on this last part of my question that my dorm friends exploded in one accord in righteous indignation, pointing and shaking their fingers at me and shouted "Liberal! Heretic!" (these were *the* dirty words in that school) and told me to "go wash your mouth."

If this incident had happened three or four centuries ago, I could no doubt have been brought to stand trial at the Spanish Inquisition, and I was glad that no school or orthodox Christians nowadays any longer practice burning heretics at the stake. Still, it is sobering to realize that there are theologians and preachers today who continue to insist that every word in the Bible is divinely inspired (meaning, every word had come out of God's mouth or otherwise dictated by God himself, *verbatim*) and, therefore, every word and every statement is inerrant. And so, the fundamental theologians would have (and seem always so able to) come up with a series of explanations to explain the unexplainable. Just a sample: "Why are there two entirely different creation stories in the Bible (Genesis Chapter One to Chapter Two, verse three, *versus* Chapter Two verse 4*ff.*)?" "Because God created one earlier, less perfect world (that's when all the dinosaurs had lived), and had to destroy it to create another, better world (where man was created in God's own image). "Why then are there two different names of god, one in Genesis Chapter One (*Elohim*, translated in English as God), and another in Genesis Chapter Two (*Yahweh*, translated in English as LORD GOD)?" "Because God's name in Chapter Two is a more personal one, since now God created Adam and Eve, and God used his personal name to establish a personal connection with them."

Hmmmmmmmmmm??? How delightfully clever are those theologians. One gets a distinct impression that they intimately know every thought in the mind of God. May we then ask if these theologians also know if God had (or had not) changed his opinion about the unclean pigs? (Actually, both Apostles Peter and Paul had changed their opinion about pigs or "unclean" foodstuffs, inferring perhaps that God could change his mind, as we do. In fact, the word "repent" was used in the Old Testament more times with God than with man, as, for instance, when God repented that He created man!) If, indeed, God first created a less perfect universe and had to destroy it in order to create a second, more perfect universe, then why did God command that the man in the first world should multiply and have dominion over all things, then changed his mind and commanded the *adama*, man (not *Adam*, a particular individual) in the second world that he should not eat the fruit of the tree of life, implying thereby that he should not multiply?

I think such problem arises from believing a story, a legend, or a *hypo*thesis, as if it is a verifiable fact. Theologians, based on statements in the Bible, steadfastly held that the earth was flat, that the earth was at the center of the universe, that there was a huge and solid celestial dome over the whole earth, and the sun and the moon and all the stars were spangled on this blue ethereal and *solid* dome. (Next time you hear the opening chorus in Haydn's *Creation*, consider the *biblical meaning* in the words "The *spacious firmament* on high, with all the *blue ethereal sky*, and *spangled heavens*, a *shining frame*, their Great Original proclaim." Here, for instance, the multiple "heavens" refers to the Paul's statement that there were *nine levels of heaven*.)

With such a dogmatic regard for Biblical statements, any opinion that proposed to the contrary was branded a heresy. Poor Nicholai Copernicus and other late medieval astronomers! Or, rather, their audacity to assume that theologians could be reasoned with to accommodate different viewpoints!

Believing an unverified hypothesis to be a fact and a truth is like saying that animals with divided hoofs, like deer, run faster than an animal with undivided hoof. Upon questioning, however, the unwavering faithful would state that a horse could run even faster if it had a divided hoof, and a cow could have become even slower if it did not have a divided hoof. Unwavering faith may give a man a sense of security of living, credence of knowledge, and esteem of self. But the danger is that, once the man accepts it as truth eternal, that *his* understanding of truth is sanctified by God, *that belief* becomes for him the source of arrogance, and an unwavering regards for all others as "heretics."

Hitler had such a hypothesis, too. He had his own idea of God and creation, and he came to believe that God created the Aryan race, a race that is superior to any other, including, of course, the Jews. And Hitler got insanely furious when an American athlete with dark complexion proved him wrong by winning a gold medal at the Olympics. Hitler did not fault his belief or his theology of the Aryan race. He blamed everyone else, including the American athlete, Jesse Owens.

All of us are familiar with the burning of Nicholai Copernicus and others at the stake, because of their viewpoints regarding the earth and heaven that were not in line with the opinion of the Church and the Bible. It took nearly four centuries for the Church to finally come to face the truth that it had erred about how God created and set in motion the heaven and earth. And it was only in recent years that the Church made the official recanting of their verdict on Galileo Galilei. We are certain that it did not take the Catholic Church, the popes, and the college of cardinals four hundred years to finally figure out that the earth was not at the center of the universe, that "*the earth does move*" (that was the last words that Galileo was alleged to murmur when he was let out of the last session of the inquisition). Rather, it was because the Church had appointed itself as the sole spokesman of God, and for the Church to admit that it had erred would be tantamount to an admission that it had made a mistake about God, or that God was misrepresented. And that would have been a big deal.

Ah, the arrogance of man! And this arrogance is at its worst when a man equates his stupidity with the infinite wisdom of God. This is the small-mindedness of man at its worst stupidity. Sadly, theologians are often the worst example of this stupidity of man.

The problem certainly is not so much with the Bible, or with the question of faith in God. The problem may very well lie in the minds of theologians who claim to know everything there is to know about God, even the mind of God. And they put on robes and prefix their surname with the title "Reverend," meaning, of course, that they are worthy to be revered, though may not be as much as God but still deserve the reverence from us the common people. And when they speak on behalf of God, no one should dare question the validity of their pronouncements.

Truthfully, I have a very difficult time understanding how a person, no matter how wise, how devout and how learned he or she may be but still a mere mortal and thus could never exceed the extent of his or her *finite* mind, would ever dare claim to comprehend the *infinite* wisdom of God. And sometimes I even think that theology, the "study of god," and denominational creeds, the dogmatic statements of man's belief formulated by the elected few, have done more harm than good to nurture man's faith in God. That is, the theology, the catechism and the creed force the people to take sides by accepting certain ideas about God that were formulated by a group of men who believed that they alone know how God thinks. Thereby these revered theologians would cause divisiveness and confrontation among the blind followers.

One only need look at the history of religion, to see how one faith divided into two, two into four, and soon god is tagged from all directions: Judaism to Christianity and Muslim, Christianity to Catholic, Eastern Orthodox, Protestant, and Protestant to Anglican, Lutheran, Methodist, Baptist. In Switzerland, John Calvin knew exactly how God saved people; God had already predestined and ordained, even before the foundation of the world was laid, that some people would be saved, and others would be condemned to eternal damnation. He was so strongly convinced of the correctness of his understanding of God's mind that he spearheaded in accusing another Christian of blasphemy, and directly caused the death of Miquel Serveto (Servetus), a Spanish theologian-physician.

The English churches were divided into high, low, and broad, and Baptists in the United States are divided into Southern, Northern and General. The memory is still fresh that, up to the recent past, Catholics and Protestants bombed one another in Ireland. A few centuries earlier, the senseless rampage of the Crusaders, all in the name of God to rid us of the Muslim infidel, was no less inhuman than that committed by the hordes of Huns (or *Xiung-Nus*, the nomads from the northern highlands of Central Asia). In India, Buddhists and Hindi have been killing one another for several centuries, and caused the death of Mahatma Ghandi, the apostle of nonviolence and believer in *anarchy* (*i.e.*, a world "without government" authority).

In modern times and for the past half a century, the world has witnessed an ever increasing conflict and campaign of terror between the Jews and Muslims, and Muslims against Muslims, all of them claiming Abraham as the father of their faiths, as if by claiming Abraham or Allah, any atrocity would be justified. Ah, would the world have been a much better place had this God-fearing Abraham had the wisdom and foresight in keeping harmony between the mothers of his two sons?! And it is infinitely distressing to realize that all this strife and killing were committed in the name of God. And we may ask, "Is God really the instigator of these tragedies? Were these, as Pope Urban the Second pronounced, truly what "God had willed it"?

Throughout the world, the Nativity passage in the Gospel of Luke is recited in countless Christian churches and private gatherings on the Christmas Eve. But I have yet to hear the reading of the passages following the Nativity story during the Christmas season. It is the passage about John the Baptizer crying in the wilderness, about how he addressed the multitudes that came out to be baptized by him (Luke 3:7-9):

> "You brood of vipers! Who warned you to flee from the
>   wrath to come?
> Bear fruits that befit repentance, and do not begin to say to
>   yourselves,
> 'We have Abraham as our father'; for I tell you, God is able
>   from these stones to raise up children of Abraham.
>
> Even now the axe is laid to the root of the trees;
>   every tree therefore that does not bear good fruit is
>   cut down and thrown into the fire."

It is a bit curious that a preacher would utter such an unkind message. But ministers today are much smarter than John to ever consider preaching such a sermon at their churches. Surely, reading such a passage is probably not a nice thing to do on Christmas eve, when all we want is to feel good about ourselves, and be assured of how good we have been, so that the jolly Santa will reward us with things we desire. For, after all, we are all the blessed children of *our* God.

Sometimes I think the problem stems from the fact that religion has become purely a business, moneymaking enterprise. Piety is assessed by the same criteria that measure social success and respectability. Priests and ministers continue to represent God's holiness and administer sacraments, knowing all the while that they have committed unspeakable sins of abomination to their youthful or female flocks. Or, the executives of the likes of Enron and financial institutions knowingly rob their fellow men of their livelihood still dress up in their Sunday best and receive cordial greetings and blessings from their ministers, all the while showing not a shred of remorse. It is as if they have trampled on the very name of God they so convincingly pretend to revere. Underneath the garb of social respectability, their cunningness and insatiable greed is not at all difficult to detect.

It is times like this that I would rather sit and eat with the poorest on the sidewalks or at the tables of Salvation Army's community kitchens, than to be in the company of those well educated, wealthy and impeccably mannered *robbers of common man*. For I have sat and eaten with the poor, desolate and neglected, at Northshore YMCA and back streets of Chicago, and have found them to be of simple and pure spirit, even without any of the acceptable social etiquette. They *are* the brothers and sisters that the prophets of the Old Testament and Jesus and his disciples had referred to. I remember a quote attributed to Leo Tolstoy, a quote worthy of our reflection:

> "I sit on a man's back, choking him and making him carry
>   me,
> and yet assure myself and others that I am very sorry for him
> and wish to ease his lot by all possible means—
> *except by getting off his back.*"

I also remember from reading Tolstoy's biography when I was in high school that, in his old age, he had abandoned everything, his family and comfortable lifestyle, and went wandering. Finally, his family (I think it was his daughter) found him in a deserted train station, far from home, and near death. I supposed Tolstoy was trying to "carry" the burden of his fellow men and to experience their suffering, instead of being carried by them and thus adding to their suffering.

What is the measure of man's piety? For me, one of the clearest statements of God's regard for man's piety is in the Book of *Isaiah*, Chapter One (*ref.* verses 10-17). Put it succinctly, God hates (*i.e.*, despises) the worship of man whose hands are "full of blood." And what is the true and acceptable offering to God? Not high social etiquette, not regular attendance at Sunday services dressed in Sunday best, not even daily reading of the Bible and reciting of denominational creeds, or regular giving of tithes and offerings. Rather, it is to "cease to do evil, learn to do good; seek justice, correct oppression, defend the fatherless, plead for the widow" (verse 17).

To carry out this commandment of God to help relieve the grief and pain of life, particularly of the poor and helpless, the early church fathers and religious offices in their collective wisdom had encouraged the dedicated faithful to serve their fellow man in three life engagements: the civil, the physical, and the spiritual. For the first are the lawyers to heal the ills of society and defend the defenseless; for the second are the physicians, to heal the ills of the human body and alleviate suffering; for the third are the ministers, to heal the ills of the human soul and bring peace and hope. And this very word "minister" connotes servitude.

And, so, as early as in the Middle Ages, the newly founded institutions of learning—the universities—began to confer doctorate degrees to these three—and only these three—disciplines: doctor of *juris prudence*; doctor of *medicine*; and doctor of *divinity*. And as they were men sworn to help relieve the pains and burdens of life and to lessen the woes of this world, they would don the monk's garb at the conclusion of their education, the garb which symbolized the servitude to God which since then has become the graduation regalia. The regalia symbolizes devotion and dedication (as virtual priests) to serve follow man, carrying out God's command that is epitomized by the life and work of the true saints such as Mother (now Saint) Teresa, Gandhi, Martin Luther King, Abraham Lincoln, and Dr. Albert Schweitzer. In their footsteps are many nameless saints of today, missionaries and non-religious-affiliated men and women who give themselves to working among the AIDs victims in Africa, and the poorest of the poor in India, Southeast Asia, and Latin America.

But, O, for the arrogance of man. With a few years of coursework and some skills in pulpit preaching, man would forget that his sworn task is to minister. After studying in college or seminary for less years than can be counted on one hand, they would now put on the ministerial garb even with three stripes on the sleeves and, suddenly, they become the anointed spokesman for the almighty and infinite God. But to think that a person could actually *complete* the study of God" in a few years to become the "Reverend" and "Doctor of Divinity"? The very notion is preposterous, ludicrous, and utterly comical at the same time. Worse, some would acquire this "god syndrome" and would stand proud and erect on the elevated platform in a superdome, a televised convention hall, or the ornate pulpit of the likes of Crystal Cathedral.

The scene is often nothing short of a commercial spectacle: pipe organ blaring, full-size orchestra and large choir performing, with limelights shining on this "man of God" to create an artificial halo. Then the Reverend Doctor SMOG (that's the acronym for **S**pokes-**M**an-**O**f-**G**od) would stand tall, high above and elevated on a platform, and deliver a gloriously crafted sermon, an articulate oracle worthy of every penny he is paid. So the Gospel proclaimed, Satan defeated, and sinners in the auditorium all cleansed and blessed, the Reverend would triumphantly return to his luxurious mansion in a chauffeur-driven limousine. I wonder how Jesus would have reacted if he walked into a service like this? Somehow, the images of the story of Jesus confronting the moneychangers at the Temple flashes through my mind.

No, there is no human being, no pope, no denominational leader, no theologian, and certainly not any of those Doctor Reverend SMOGS, who can ever claim or even pretend to have been anointed as the inerrant spokesman for God. The best one can ever hope to be in the service of God's vineyard is to first humble himself in recognition of his limitation and sinfulness, then to minister to the needs of God's people. Like the prophet Isaiah, even after many years of service, he would confess that he was "of unclean lips, and dwells among the people of unclean lips." Standing before the Holiest God, man could do no otherwise than to confess his inadequacy (*cf.* the "inaugural vision" of prophet Isaiah, in *Isaiah* 6:1-8). Maybe there was something in my father's peculiar motto for his ministry, after all: "*Minister to the people in poor churches. For, there, you will see the will of God more clearly.*"

One Monday afternoon, over four decades ago, Dr. Page Kelly, an eminent Biblical scholar at Southern Baptist Theological Seminary, invited the students in his class on the *Book of Isaiah* to share their ministry experience and personal reflection from the previous weekend. One by one, the divinity-degree program students shared their encounters, narrating stories of their previous weekend's achievements and difficulties. As I was the only non-theology major in the class, I sat and listened in silence. In different words describing a wide range of encounters and feelings, they expressed more or less the same, shared sense of frustration, that their week's preparation, preaching and earnest invitation to the people to respond to God's calling went unheeded and brought little tangible fruition. While the students spoke, I watched the countenance of Dr. Kelly, an otherwise utterly unassuming, humble and sincere man, with gentle smile that seemed never to fade from his face, who until then had been quietly listening to students' reports, gradually turn sober. He patiently waited until the last student spoke, walked to the front of the desk, and slowly uttered the following words which I will long remember.

> "Do you think the ministry is so difficult, that your labor often goes unrewarded? The truth is that
> God's ministry is *not difficult*; it is *IMPOSSIBLE*.
> What do you think you are?
> How could we think that we, the *finite man*, will ever be capable of doing God's work?
> It is only by the grace of God that we have been called to minister.
> Only by recognizing this grace will we see our inadequacy.
> In humbling ourselves, we will see that ministry is *not a job, but a privilege*.
> Never forget that '*Many are called, but few are chosen.*'"

Beethoven's *Ninth Symphony* is famous for its earliest use of human voices in an otherwise purely instrumental composition. And the music of the last movement, the 'choral' movement, has been made singularly famous because it was put on a disc that was sent out in the spaceship some years ago, to travel to the outer limits of the universe, in the (most unlikely) event that some intelligent beings are out there in deep cosmic void and, some years or centuries from now, the unearthly creatures would capture our tiny spaceship and would listen to the disc that may still play the theme of "*Ode to Joy.*" This choral movement is based on the poem of Friedrich von Schiller about the dignity and brotherhood of man. Perhaps a brief remark will help one appreciate a bit more about the intent of Beethoven's music.

The First Movement describes man's uncertain search—more like groping in the dark—for an answer to the question of the meaning of life.

An answer comes in the Second Movement. It is a *scherzo*, a wild dance that seems to suggest that life is for "singing, dancing, drinking, and being merry," in other words, a licentious living. But suddenly the music is interrupted, as if to deny that wild living is not the answer to the meaning of life.

Another answer comes in the Third Movement. Unlike the wild music of the Second Movement, this is a solemn and moving hymn, suggesting that man should find the answer in faith in God. But, even the beautiful hymn is abruptly denied.

Then, the Fourth Movement begins with the same questioning music that was heard in the First Movement, and the themes from the Second and the Third Movements reappear, only to be dismissed. Man is still groping for an answer to the meaning of life. Then, gradually, almost rising up from a tranquil void, a Gregorian chant-like melody is intoned, first by a single instrument part, then joined by other parts. Then an orchestral punctuation, and a human voice, the baritone solo, intones:

> "Oh, brothers, not these tones (the songs in movements II
>   and III)" but, rather,
> "... by God's magic of love is all mankind united ..."

Music continues to swell, with choruses, tenor solo, quartet, and the final joining of the four soloists and the full chorus leading to a thunderous and breathtaking climax. Schiller's poem is commonly referred to as the "*Ode to Joy*," but I think it should be called "*The Triumphal Song of Brotherly Love of Mankind.*"

What is the meaning in Beethoven's music set to Schiller's poem? It is this: Man's salvation is not in wild and licentious living, not even in the pious religious shrines and devout lifestyle, but in man's deeds of love toward his fellow man. Without brotherly love, we are no better than primitive creatures, fighting for survival and trampling fellow creatures to get on top. Without brotherly love, there is no God (that is, God will have nothing to do with loveless creatures), for such man is no longer in the image of God. Without brotherly love and genuine compassion for fellow man, there will never be Man as we hope we can all be, or are capable of becoming.

11

A Scene from the Modern Tower of Babel

I rose early the morning of Saturday, March 21, for a trip to Taiwan where I was invited to give a series of lectures at several colleges. I literally sneaked out of the house, fearful of waking up my nearly five-year-old son who had been threatening me that I wasn't going anywhere without him. I changed planes at San Francisco for a non-stop flight to Taipei, and I found myself seated next to an elderly couple who introduced themselves as being from the San Francisco area, that they were taking their very first trip to the Far East and Southeast Asia. The gentleman was a retired accountant and had worked for a while for his church mission board (Christian Church). Mr. and Mrs. Ohler were genuinely excited about the trip, and told me that they had read a number of booklets that introduce the places they were to visit: Singapore, Bangkok, and Hong Kong. They asked me if I was American-born, and I was flattered, for I thought that surely they would detect my ever-present accent. I told them that I was born and raised in Taiwan, and actually had finished college there before coming to America, and that I had been living in Texas for about twenty years. That way, I believed they might perhaps understand and excuse me if they began to notice my accent later in our conversation, taking it as a *peculiar* brand of Texas accent.

We talked for nearly an hour, and they seemed genuinely appreciative of the information and tidbits I shared with them, about the people and customs of Southeast Asia, and places—those tourist Meccas—they might want to remember as worth visiting. Our conversation broke off for a while but, a few hours into the flight, they mentioned their puzzlement over the changing of the date going to the Far East; you loose a day going from the United States to the Far East, and gain back a day when coming the other way. I briefly mentioned to them the international date line in the middle of the Pacific Ocean, but chose not to go into too much detail, as I didn't want them to get an impression—especially before going to Singapore, Bangkok, and Hong Kong swarmed with loud Chinese—that all Chinese are talkative and show-offs.

As I resettled myself into a more comfortable position in the seat, preparing for a long, long flight—some twelve to fourteen hours from San Francisco to Taipei, where the plane would refuel before taking the Ohlers to Hong Kong—my thoughts began to wander, all starting from the point of this international date line that my next-seat travel companions found puzzling, and about this "the East is East, and the West is West" question. To begin with, for example, here I was, going to the Far East but, in order to reach the *East*, I would need to travel *west*ward. My thoughts even went back some thirty years ago, to the time I left my home; I flew *east*ward to reach the most *west*ern new frontier of the Western world, the United States.

I had just graduated from college, and my parents had to borrow money to pay for my passage to the States and the first semester tuition and board. For a less expensive flight, I boarded a plane that was converted from a U.S. cargo plane. It had to make an overnight stop at Guam in an upgraded old army barrack on Wake Island, then at Hawaii and, finally, arrived at Oakland, California. The entire trip took three full days. And I learned that it was somewhere between Wake Island and Hawaii Islands that the date changed by crossing the international date line drawn north to south. Of course, in crossing this date line, there was no noticeable change or any call to attention, no sonic boom, not even a whimper. For this is a purely man-made demarcation line, just like this invisible line distinguishing the Eastern and Western cultures.

Actually, this man-made date line is drawn from the North Pole to the South Pole, right on the 180° meridian line, going down just west of another U.S. territorial island in the Pacific, Midway Island. This line, however, is not at all straight; in the northern end, it swivels around to conveniently put Alaska and the Aleutian Islands into the same date zone with the U.S. continent. It then goes down straight along the 180° meridian line southward over the Pacific Ocean until it reaches a few archipelagos in the south Pacific, where the line bends eastward to put these islands in the same date zone with Australia. I suppose this 180° meridian is the most convenient line that can be drawn on this world, since this date demarcation line cuts through virtually no land area and thus would cause the least amount of dispute or confusion among people living on adjacent lands.

The drawing of this date line also can be appreciated from another perspective. This is the farthest point from zero-degree meridian. Let me explain. To the *west* of this 180° meridian are the *east*ern meridian lines of 179°, 178°, 177°, *etc.*, while to the *east* of this 180° meridian are the *west*ern meridian lines of 179°, 178°, 177°, *etc.*, also in continually decreasing number, and the eastern and western meridian lines finally would meet at the so-called zero-degree point. This 0° meridian line is at the Greenwich Observatory, a little way southeast from the center of London, England. To put it another way, the *east*ern meridian lines begin at and move *east*ward from Greenwich, and the *west*ern lines move to the *west* of Greenwich, all the way around the world up to east 180° and west 180°, where the twain meet exactly half way around the world from Greenwich and, bingo, you have the same 180° *east/west* meridian line which is the international date line.

Let's put it yet another way. There are two north-to-south drawn lines where the east and west truly meet: 0° and 180° meridian lines. One is in the very western part of Europe, going from England southward through parts of France and Spain, down the western part of the Africa continent to the Port of Accra, just missing the famous (?) Timbuktu to the west by a few miles. (Now you know where Timbuktu is the next time you invoke this town's honorable name.) The other is in the Pacific Ocean, literally in the middle of nowhere. The ancient Greeks made Athens, the capital of Greece, the central point of reference for east and west, while modern (or Western) geographers put that reference point at the city of Greenwich, England. Athens had temples where the *lunarians* (the priests) offered sacrifices and prayers to the sky over that City of the Gods. Greenwich has the observatory where the modern *lunarians* (the star-gazers) still peer into the sky night after night. Not much has changed in these past two millennia, really.

Thinking about and counting all those imaginary lines over the surface of the earth was more soothing than a lullaby or counting sheep, and I fell asleep over some meridian lines over the Pacific Ocean. By the time the plane landed at Taipei International Airport, it was already late afternoon, Sunday March 22 (the early morning hours of the *same date* in Texas), and I thought of my son, and hoped that he was not angry with me for leaving him behind. And I found myself in a wholly westernized and ultra modern airport facility except the fact that nearly all the faces I saw were Eastern.

For the following few days I gave lectures, speaking mostly about Western music to Eastern musicians whose interests and orientations are more Western than Eastern inclined. I was treated most princely and, whenever I had a choice, I would always ask for Eastern food, the kind even the best Asian restaurants in Texas would be unable to provide. One evening I received a call from Mr. Li Julin, my elementary school classmate. He also was the best man at our wedding and, even after all these years and without much direct contact, we still felt a very close kindred spirit. For we were *the minority* (of three) in the otherwise all-Japanese elementary school class.

Without asking me, Mr. Li took me to a Japanese restaurant, one of his favorite eateries, so he told me later. Sitting at the counter where all sorts of raw, utterly fresh sea foods in an impressive array were displayed in a glass case, my host ordered for each of us one personalized dish after another (I was glad I didn't have to share) and, after about half a dozen or so, I lost count. Actually I was busy eating than counting, and a bystander would probably describe my manner as "wolfing" than "eating." I would not belabor on this by listing or describing the food I had that night, for fear of being excommunicated for behavior most unbecoming of a Texan. Still, I would like to mention just one: the *uni* (pronounced OO-NEE, both short syllable), and suggest that you would inquire about this particular dish the next time you visit a Japanese restaurant.

Still, I must admit to you, dear reader, that the purest and the best of Japanese seafood culinary offerings simply defy any Western description. And, as the Taiwanese aboriginal men had worried if Jesus' arms would be as hairy as those of Dr. Dickson (see [ONE] "THE EAST IS EAST, AND THE WEST IS WEST, OR IS IT?"), I too worry whether such a seafood feast would be available at the heavenly tables. In a private and selfish moment, I would even pray that heaven's cuisine would be more Eastern than Western, preferably Chinese or Japanese but, please, OH PLEASE! not the heart-burning Tex-Mex type.

Near the noon hour on Sunday, March 29, I arrived at the airport for the flight home. After checking in the luggage, we were advised that the plane would be some four to six hours delayed due to mechanical problems at the point of origin—Bangkok. A little while later, another announcement came, informing the already uneasy passengers that the flight was canceled for that day, that the rescheduled flight would leave the *following day, two hours before* the *regularly-scheduled time for the same flight*. (A fine example of an oxymoron.)

We were given meal and hotel vouchers, and were transported to Airport Hotel in the nearby city of Taoyuan. We were also given a free three-minute international call to inform our concerned parties at the point of destination (in my case my ever anxious wife and my impetuous son). The accommodations were more than adequate, and I feasted on another sumptuous Chinese dinner in a spacious and meticulously serviced dining hall.

The following morning we were all at the airport by ten o'clock, and the boarding area was overflowing with a very anxious crowd, including the new group of passengers just arrived from Bangkok on the *same scheduled flight one day late*. There were Chinese, Koreans, Japanese, Indians, Filipinos, Malaysians, a few German and French passengers and, of course, the ever-present American tourists. I had little problem identifying the nationalities of these people since I speak a little bit of each of all these languages except Indian, but the Indians are easily distinguishable even without hearing them speak.)

Then, the most improbable happened. The announcement came through the loudspeaker that the plane had some mechanical problems again! An unofficial explanation was that a bird (or birds) flew into one of the engines when it was landing. And I thought, "Well, that's *just for the birds!*" (in English, I think). Maybe a half-hour delay but no more than two hours, so the agent at the counter announced, trying to console the anxious passengers and to calm the irritations quite visible on the facial expressions and voices of the tourists.

A number of airline personnel came into the waiting area with carts, and we were served free coffee and a "four-course" lunch all neatly packed in a fancy *bento* box (a Japanese term which, in Chinese, is *bian-dang*, literally means "convenience" that had come to mean "conveniently" boxed lunch). "This sure beats the meager one-tray plane meal," I tried to console myself. But before I was even finished with the lunch, word was spread quickly—never publicly announced—that the plane might be grounded for another day, but there were some forty to fifty seats available on another regularly scheduled flight.

The ensuing stampede from the restaurants, shopping arcades, and the waiting area, and the pandemonium—more like shoveling and shouting matches all at once—converging at the counter next to the boarding gate were almost too frightful to watch. I have never before heard the frustrated and angry shouting in multiple languages all at once and increasingly in *molto crescendo e tempo agitato* ("much increasing loudness and in agitated speed"), pathetic and hilarious at the same time, exhibiting the worst of human nature.

Until then, I had somehow come to expect that Westerners were more polite and civilized, courteous, orderly and considerate of others. But the scene in front of my very eyes proved me completely wrong. I was particularly dismayed (perhaps "feeling nauseated" was a more accurate description) in watching some well-dressed Western tourists and business people behaving as if their being Non-Asian had some divinely endowed social caste higher than the shorter, less well-dressed and less pale-skinned Asians. And I had to turn my eyes away from one middle-age American lady who was literally cursing and manhandling a couple of elderly Chinese ladies who got in her way. Of course, Asians, too, weren't behaving any better, except the fact that they didn't *dare* cuss or push away the Westerners. I was witnessing a reenactment of the historical Biblical scene at the Tower of Babel, when God in His infinite wisdom had decided to confound the language of man, and everyone began shouting at the top of his or her voice in order to be heard. Of course, no one could hear, let alone understand, what was being shouted, because everyone else also was busy shouting with the full force of his/her lungs all at the same time and in different languages.

To "rationally" resolve the virtually impossible situation, the agents decided that the holders of the airlines' **PREMIER MILEAGE PLUS** cards (of United Airlines) were to be given priority-seating opportunity. Although I had just such a card for a few years, I had never taken it with me on my prior trips. But, for some reason—call it a premonition—just before I left home, I had tucked it in my wallet. I pulled the card out and waved it overhead, and soon I was among the chosen few. A few minutes later, my name was called, and I boarded the plane. At long, long last, the plane left the runway, nearly two hours later than the *scheduled* time of *that* flight. After getting on board the flight that was already one day and several hours later than my own initial itineraries, I suddenly realized that all my luggage was not on *this* flight, but would be on the other, further delayed plane, and began to wonder how I was going to get my son to understand when I saw him that his presents would be arriving at least another day late.

A few hours into the homeward flight, I walked to the rear of the cabin and looked out the window. (Those were the "good ol' days" when passengers on board were allowed to wander the length of the plane.) Early evening shadow was over the gray ocean far below, and I reflected on the scene I had left behind a few hours earlier. From high above the terrestrial planes, above all the hustle and bustle of earthly concerns, the angry shouts and pushes of men and women and their rude manners and hurtful curses that not only were heard at the airport but could be heard at so many corners of the pathways along life's journey, seem all so senseless, so trivial and inconsequential. I thought of the minuteness of man, small not in terms of measurable stature but of mind and heart. And I thought how little our education, upbringing, our cultures and all the ethical codes written and unwritten, actually and effectively alter and ennoble our primitive nature. Professional or lay, young or old, man or woman, Eastern or Western, we all respond to life's real situations exactly alike. Perhaps we—myself included—are no better or higher than any other "lowly" creatures. We are too much alike in more ways than we care to admit. And we, whether Easterners or Westerners, are not—perhaps never will be—nobler than our all-too-human limitations. The really sad part of it all is not so much that we are limited but, rather, that too often we are quick to boast our capacity to comprehend the "truth" as whatever we conveniently define it to be, and to believe that somehow our cultural heritages, our enlightened society, and our education have made us a better creature, a nobler caste of people than "other" kinds of human beings. And only on rare occasions do we face the true greatness of human character, be it moral, ethical, educational, philosophical or religious, and we are forced to bow our heads in humility of spirit and shamefulness of arrogance.

It was during my sophomore year in high school that my parents "adopted" a young man by the name of A-hui, from a small town south of Hualien. It was a period of time when our family's financial situation was anything but bright, as we lived off a small income from the land my parents leased out for rice farming, and none of my parents held any salaried positions. To supplement the family income, my parents bought milk goats, and we became goat-milk producers. Every day, my father and I would get up in the wee hours of the morning, and we would milk the goats, and I became very good at it and could milk faster and squeeze more milk out of each goat than my father. After boiling it, we would bottle the milk, and I would make deliveries on my bicycle to our circle of customers, all before I walked several miles up the hill to school. Since I was in earnest preparation for college entrance exams, my parents relieved me of the chore and engaged this jovial young man to assist in our little goat-milk business.

A-hui was a couple of years younger than I, but was tall, healthy and strong, and utterly innocent, quite proud of his physical dexterity. And he was particularly proud of his swimming ability, boasting to us more than once that he had swum back and forth the full length of the lake in his mountain village.

One day, I learned that he had never seen the ocean, and was most anxious to go to the seashore. On our way to the beach, he again talked about his swimming ability, and said excitedly, "I heard that the ocean is really big. But I will show you how good a swimmer I am. I will swim to the center of the ocean, and swim back." I told him that ocean was much, much bigger than the lake in his village and, besides, there were big, big waves. "Oh, the lake has waves too, when the wind is blowing," he answered, not at all concerned with my description of the ocean.

A little while later, we stood at the dock on the beach looking out to the open sea. There, he stood motionless, transfixed, with both his eyes and mouth wide open, totally dumbfounded. The vastness of the Pacific Ocean, with its dancing spray and the deafening roars of the unrelenting pounding waves, its vast expanse and the endless horizon stretching to the end of the sky, were simply too much for his small, mountain-village mind to grasp. He literally coiled back into himself, walked quietly with me and returned home, without even wetting his feet in the ocean which, just a little while earlier, he had boasted of conquering.

12

The Tower of Babel and Language of Man

One day a few months after we moved to Texas and I began teaching at the University of North Texas (Denton, TX), I stopped at a gas station on the service road of Interstate 35, a few blocks from the campus. As I was maneuvering the hose, I saw a large white Cadillac convertible pull into the station. The car drove up to the "full service" lane, and the gentleman asked the station attendant to fill his gas tank, check the oil, and clean the windshield. Our eyes met, and we both smiled. The gentleman, about my height (5'6"), perhaps only a few years older than I, and wearing a wide brimmed Texas hat, got out of his car and approached me.

"Howdy," he said, now with a broader smile, and asked me if I was a student at the university. I replied and said that I actually had just started teaching at the university.

"Oh, you are one of those college professors!"

"I suppose I am."

"Do you like teaching?"

"Yes, I hope so."

"Do you like Texas?"

"I think we do. We just moved down here from Chicago, and we think Texans are very friendly."

And we stood there and carried on a pleasant conversation even though we had already paid for our gas. It was a novel experience for me, since I know that in Chicago or Detroit (where I held my first full-time teaching position), people just don't start talking to strangers only because you happen to be at the gas pump at the same time.

This gentleman seemed a genuinely friendly sort, and I couldn't detect any pretense. I figured that he was just curious about this Asian university professor. He asked me what I taught, where did I come from, if I was married, to a Chinese or American, had any children, and other "just friendly" sorts of inquisitive questions that I didn't mind at all answering. Then he told me that he didn't get any college education; in fact he didn't even get to finish high school. "But I have done OK, quite OK," he said. Then his smile got even broader and asked, "*Have* you ever *saw* a Texas checkbook before?" I confessed that I had not, that I didn't know checkbooks in Texas were any different from checkbooks in other states.

"I'll show-*ya*," he said, and pulled out from the back pocket of his tight beige jeans what I first thought was a regular checkbook. He opened the cover of the leather folder, and I saw that inside was a stack of mint-condition one-hundred-dollar bills, gummed at the top end, conveniently, ready for peeling off. "Wow, that's *something*!" I let out an exclamation of genuine surprise, and he smiled again. We chatted for a few more minutes, and I congratulated him on his life's success and happiness, and we waved friendly good-byes and drove off.

While driving to the campus, I thought how precious this Texas *country* gentleman was, unassuming, friendly, and yet deeply proud of what he is, with or without higher education or his Texas checkbook. And I also thought how precious language is. Here we were two total strangers, from opposite sides of the world, with cultural and educational backgrounds as far apart. Yet we communicated amicably, candidly, as if we had been friends for many years.

Texans are, in some ways, an adorable people. Behind that tall and proud exterior is a personality of child-like innocence. Texans are carefree and friendly, so long as you don't step on their toes. They are a natural lover of freedom and, I suppose, this personality is nurtured by the heritage of living in a wide open prairie land thousands of acres wide, as far as the eyes can see in every direction. And it is utterly flat; there seems nothing in their way. And I understand why Texas cowboys are *how* they are. For I have seen real cowboys, the ranch hands, shopping in grocery stores, and noticed on two occasions when I went to the store late in the evening that all they bought were a couple of six-packs of beer and a few pieces of thick steak. And I imagined how, after a hard day's work, they would relax, stretching out on the grassy knoll under the tree, with steaks on the open fire and beer cans in their hands, and with not a worry in the world. And I remembered well how eager we, as high school students in Taiwan, were to learn the English songs, how much we loved to sing the first cowboy song, and thought how romantic it would be to experience a life

> "… Where seldom is heard a discouraging word,
> And the skies are not cloudy all day.
> Home, home on the range, …"

When in 1991 I visited China for the first time in my life, I was told that *MARLBOROUGH* was the best selling brand of cigarettes in China, because the picture on the huge advertisement boards high up in so many street corners depicts a cowboy sitting on horseback looking out into a wide, open space. Apparently, the image of complete freedom that cigarette ad so effectively portrays, is something that people living in the overcrowded land, where the big brothers are always watching your every move, would yearn for, and long to identify with.

Ah, Texas! Driving a pickup truck, carrying a shotgun or two on the gun-rack on the rear window of your truck, and you can literally take off for anywhere you wish to go, on the highway system that is more extensive than any other state in the union. And there is no doubt that the sense of being free from all concerns plays a significant part in the shaping of the unique persona of Texans. A few years after moving to Texas, I even bought myself a Ford half-ton pickup truck, and tried to see how it would really feel to be a Texan. But that was as far as my "Texas Experiment" went. I just couldn't bring myself to wearing boots (they were too expensive, for one thing) and a ten-gallon hat (over a five-foot-and-six-inch body?), for I know how *silly* I would look. And putting a shotgun and gun-rack on the rear window was simply out of the question. For I knew all too well that I would NEVER LOOK like a *native* Texan, no matter how hard I might try.

Texas is truly big, and Texans have big hearts. They are often the first to respond to calls for rescue or aid to distressed people on the farthest sides of the world. At the same time, that is about as far as their natural extent of the world seems. When you live under the big and blue and cloudless sky, in the middle of an open prairie where you might be a hundred miles from your nearest neighbors, you would likely begin to feel that you are almost alone in the center of this big wide world. In fact, Texas is the world. In Texas, we have Athens and Paris, Italy, Rome, Canton, and even Corinth and Palestine, all within easy driving distance in your pickup truck. And we are friendly; even the name of our State means "friendly" (*tejas* in Spanish). And we are open-minded; one can even carry on a friendly conversation with a Chinese professor at a roadside gas station.

Shortly after we moved to Texas (1972), I sent a package to Taiwan. Talking about a slow boat to Shanghai; it took nearly two months to arrive. My friend wrote me that the package was very late in arriving, and that it had [THAILAND] stamped on it. Apparently, the postal clerk sent the package intended for TAIWAN to THAILAND instead. For the big-hearted Texas postal clerk, TAIWAN, THAILAND, or even TEHRAN all sounded alike. Living in a big state like Texas, and in a big country like America, there is a distinct tendency that we don't feel any urgent need to know the rest of the world, that we would rather regard them as small territories "somewhere out there" in the fringes of our big Texas prairie.

Still, language is a wonderful and amazing thing. Language can break down barriers between peoples, and help to diminish the biases. Language can transport us beyond time barriers, allowing us to "talk" to and understand the thoughts of the people who had lived centuries or even millennia ago. Hence it is doubly sad to think that this same, wonder-working vehicle of communication can also become an obstacle in the more urgent moment of communication between two people who don't speak exactly alike. Then, the wonderful words of man become the vehicle of *mis*communication, from which *mis*understanding and even hatred may result. This is because man has a tendency to be *lingo-centric* (as well as *ego-centric* and *ethno-centric*). When someone talks "funny" or doesn't understand what we are saying, we quickly label that person a *nitwit*. We surely would like nothing better than for the whole world to speak English, or at least good Texan, and that would indeed be glorious.

So we look into a future time when the day will come when English finally and rightfully becomes the world language, when there would be no longer any need for anyone to learn any other language. Then the world will be restored to what it was before the time of the Tower of Babel, before God somehow felt that it was not good that people were getting smarter, that he needed to confound their language, so that each would not be able to understand the other. So the people who "babble" unintelligently were called the people from the tower of "Babel"—the babblers.

I could never figure out why God felt the need to confound the language of man. (My theology professor had once explained this point in his own convincing way, but I still like to pose this same question whenever I get a chance.) But I know that, with the multitude of languages, arrogant man found yet another vehicle to help him feel superior to others who just babble. When Christopher Columbus set sail toward "east" India, he had among his crew on board a scholar of the Hebrew language. Why? Because the devout Columbus believed that, since Hebrew was God's language, and was mankind's first and only language before God decided to confound man's language, therefore, in far-away lands, this original language might still be spoken, or at least could be used to communicate with the natives there. We suspect that Columbus had found out otherwise, because he did not bring another Hebrew language scholars on board in his subsequent voyages.

Like Columbus, we the English speaking people regard ours to be the best language, and some of us would even believe that the *King James* (version of the) Bible is *the* inspired word of God, as if God speaks only English, that a Bible in any other language is not quite the right kind of Bible. (I like the way Professor Higgins put it, in *MY FAIR LADY*, "English is a *noble* language, the *language of Shakespeare and Milton* ...") And the descendants of the European West would regard the Chinese and Japanese as reading their Bible backwards, writing in their funny chicken scratches starting from the back. And, when we can't understand what the people are saying in other languages, we would say, "It's *Greek* to me" or "It's *Chinese* to me," and would call these "other" people *nitwits* when they fail to understand what we are saying.

Actually, *we* are the *nitwits*. The word *nitwits* came from a Dutch word "*niet weet*" which simply means "I don't understand," a natural response to American tourists who insist on asking directions in English, who believe that all Dutch *should* understand English. A story has it that Captain Cook had a native assistant with him one day when he was surveying exotic animals in Australia. Captain Cook halted in surprise when a large animal crossed their path hopping. Excited, the Captain asked "What was that?" The assistant answered "*kan-ga-roo*," and Captain Cook carefully jotted the sound of this new beast's name down in his notebook. He did not realize that what the assistant actually said was "*I don't know*."

Forget about *niet weet* and forget about *kangaroo*. We Americans are one people who are the least capable of speaking languages other than our own. And we are the least knowledgeable of the rest of the world, except some bits and pieces of information we get from the abbreviated "international" news on TV in the evening. We Americans are the one people not *required* in all of twelve years public school education to become proficient—be able to read, speak and write—in at last one other language. Yet we refuse to admit that we have the most biased perspectives of people in other parts of the world. And we send emissaries to China, to Japan, or elsewhere, or government agents to negotiate important political and economic agenda, the people who couldn't even hold the chopstick straight, let alone speak the language of these countries with any measurable degree of fluency and comprehension. And we like to poke fun at those foreign diplomats, delegates and students, that they speak English with silly accents and all the most laughable grammatical errors.

A colleague of mine at the university once told me that his Korean composition student came into his studio one day for the weekly lesson, and was most apologetic. "She said she was sorry because she didn't work very hard this past week, and she only 'wrote two *shiit* of music.'" A piano faculty related to me about his student who went to a contest. "'How did you do?' I asked her, and she said, 'I don't really know. I just *prayed* and *prayed* (instead of played and played), and the people *crapped* and *crapped* (instead of clapped and clapped).'" And this colleague roared in laughter most uncontrollably, and I joined in laughter in a gesture of collegial etiquette.

I suppose this sort of thing happens everywhere; Chinese laugh at Western missionaries trying hopelessly to negotiate the tonal inflection in the Chinese spoken language, often with comical results, and Americans laugh at Asian students and government delegates who mispronounce R for L, and *vice versa*. Not long ago, a concert of a Chinese traditional instrument ensemble (from Kaohsiung, Taiwan) was given at Dallas' Meyerson Symphony Center, and I was asked to give a short introduction about the unique features of Chinese instruments. Before I spoke, a diplomatic *attaché* representing the Taiwan government's Cultural Office in Houston gave an official greeting. In extending a warm welcome on behalf of the government, he said "the *whore* of Dallas and Fort Worth Chinese community wants to thank" the citizens of the metroplex in attending this special concert. [Of course he meant "*whole*" instead of "*whore*"; he really should have used the word "entire" instead.] We may politely smile, or chuckle, or even laugh out loud, and such reactions are regarded as innocent and harmless. But on other occasions and in much more serious situations, mispronunciation and misinterpretation may cause—and actually have caused—disastrous consequences.

It was toward the end of World War II, and U.S. planes were sending daily air-raid sorties to Japanese cities. Then, a few days prior to dropping atomic bombs in Hiroshima and Nagasaki, the U.S. government sent a secret *communique* about its plans to employ the bombs, and to warn the Japanese government of their horrendous destructive force of unprecedented scale, and requested the Japanese high command to seriously consider. The Japanese high command met, discussed, and sent back the reply:

"We shall '*moku-satsu*' your warning." The U.S. translator(s) interpreted this word to mean "refuse," and the order was given to drop the atomic bomb.

Too bad for Japan and the countless thousands of civilians who lost their lives in a split second of a blinding flash of light, and for another countless thousands who had to suffer irrevocable physical suffering and psychological anguish for years following that fateful instance. It is agonizingly sad to think that *that* horrendous human suffering might have been avoided had the US translators known that there were several different meanings to the word "*moku-satsu*," among them is one that the Japanese often used to "save face" when defeat was all too inevitable but, the pride of *samurai* would not allow them to say the word "*make-mashita*" (I am defeated). The best translation of the inference in this word *moku-satsu* might be something like "[I will have to] *ignore*" (which may be equated to a *tacit admission of defeat and acceptance of the inevitable*). The tragedy was the result of *mis*communication on two levels: One was that the American translators were trained to translate the Japanese *words*, but they were never trained to comprehend the *language*. Two, to comprehend the Japanese language, one must have lived among the Japanese, immersed in the culture, and *experience the living language*. For there is so much intricacy of meaning and inference in Japanese spoken language, arguably the most esoteric of all the languages in the world. And Japanese high command did not expect that Americans were not capable of appreciating the inference in Japanese language, and the American command and the translators certainly were not equipped to comprehend the same. The words were taken—or, in this case, *mis*taken—for granted, and one of the greatest of human massacres was allowed to happen.

While I dare not for a moment claim myself to be a linguist, I know that the Japanese language is the most subtle, esoteric, private and "hidden" of all languages, and it is nearly impossible for an accurate "word-to-word translation" from Japanese to English (or to any European languages). It is the only language (I know) that does not require a subject or a verb in a "sentence" and, as a result, the whole "sentence" would become completely nebulous if it is trans-literated. Too complicated to cite sentence examples, but we may look at a few common phrases: Do you know that "*moshi-moshi*" (as in "hello" when making a telephone call) literally means "if ..., if ..."? or "*sayo-nara*" (as in saying "good bye" in parting with friends) literally means "if so, then ..."? Anyone who had spent any time in Japan would know that, without doubt, the most useful (and the most frequently used) word in the entire Japanese conversation, including greeting, is "*doh-moh*." But this word simply defies translation. The closest it comes is "very much." But "very much" what? Well, the *mystique* of the Japanese (arts, language, personality, all things Japanese) is in the *unspoken part*, unverbalized but clearly inferred and well understood (by the Japanese) in the context of the conversation. Thus, "*doh-moh*" could be "*doh-moh sumimasen*" ("very much unfinished" to mean "very sorry" and, hence, an apology), or *doh-moh ari-gatoh gozaimashita* ("very much difficult to possess" to mean "things very hard to come by" and, hence, conveying a grateful acceptance, as "thank you"). Whatever needs to be said, it is clearly inferred by the situation and, therefore, needs not be said explicitly.

It is, in other words, an *art* form and *poetry* in language, where impression and inference is more important than the precise words being enunciated. But, of course, the practical-minded and grammatics-obsessed Western mind finds such language annoyingly imprecise and defective. And the *poetic*-minded and *metaphysics*-inclined Eastern mind finds the European language rigidly confining. Why always get so particular about the article, the tense, gender, number, and all other grammatical and idiomatic constraints? Do you have to bend low to check to see if a tiger chasing after you is male or female before you could call out for help? I don't care if French do; Asians are much smarter, and couldn't care less about the beast's gender when one's life is at stake.

But why, even among Asian languages, is the Japanese language so peculiar and ambiguous? Like the gender of a tiger *versus* my own life, it has to do with the "art" of survival. In the history of Japan, there was a long period preceding the *Meiji ishin* (political reformation for restoration of imperial power under Emperor Meiji) in the second half of the nineteenth century. For nearly a thousand years, the entire Japan was in a state of constant and continuous warfare among regional warlords. It was during this *bakufu* or *feudal* period that the *caste of samurai* was created. *Samurai*, literally means "one who serves," were the retainers of the powerful warlords and thus were conferred the special privilege of carrying swords, in exchange for their unconditional pledge of loyalty, even unto death. To supply the warlords and their enormous ranks of samurai, the rice farmers became virtual slaves, giving up everything and getting nothing in return except spitefulness and abuse. The farmers did not have any right, whether it was the land they till, the straw huts they live in, or their very lives. And for even the slightest of impropriety in word or deed, samurai had the unwritten right to take the life of a farmer or a commoner. (There is just such a scene early in the movie in James Clavell's *Shôgun*; a fisherman lost his head because he did not bow his head low enough and, thus, it was regarded as a posture of defiance in the presence of a *samurai* captain.)

What would or could the poor rice farmers or fishermen do when you know that the smallest of misstep in word or deed could get your heads rolling off your shoulders? That's when the axiom "silence is golden" was at its most precious worth. You speak little or nothing, or when you must speak, you do so in as utterly *nebulous* way possible. In other words, you speak but you say almost nothing, and the meaning is left to the other party, to let him "hear" whatever he wants to hear.

American businessmen get excited doing business in Japan, when a business deal seems finally to get nailed down. The next day he would bring the prepared document expecting his Japanese counterpart to sign. The Japanese counterpart appears puzzled, stating that the deal had not been agreed on the day before. "But you said '*Soh desu*' (yes, it is so)," the American would insist. "Oh, I am so sorry, but you are mistaken," the Japanese rep would beg to differ. "All I said was "*Soh de-sho neh?*" (may be it is so, perhaps). You see, it is not a firm *yes* and neither is it a definite *no*. It is more like "do you think so?" and, thereby, leaving room for reinterpretation and renegotiation. Ah, that wonderful little nonsense-syllable word "*neh*" (actually, it is not a word) at the end of a phrase (rarely a complete sentence)! "*Neh!*" is the escape valve that frees all the preceding words from obligatory binding. Asians—and Japanese in particular—are very cunning and manipulative negotiators. They are like over-ripened fruits; soft outside but, inside, there is a very *hard nut that is difficult to crack.*

In contrast, Americans are, well, Americans. They are, to borrow the phrase the exasperated British soldiers used to describe the GIs, "overpaid, over-sexed, and over here!" To which, I might add "over-hasty and A-OK" to get things done. Americans seldom take time to try to understand—let alone appreciate—the intricacies of the language of other people, yet we the Americans expect other people to think and act as we do. And when they don't, we get impatient and become quick to regard others as being unfit to be our equals.

One of the most glaring examples of this U.S.-centric attitude toward the rest of the world is the requirement that all U.S. schools—high schools and universities—are bound in giving admission to foreign students. It is called **TOEFL** (**T**est **O**f **E**nglish as a Foreign **Language**). Until a few years ago, the passing score for TOEFL was set at 450. Since then, the score has been raised to 500, then to 550, which the college officials regard as the mark of higher academic standards of their schools. I have taught at the University of North Texas for over twenty years (since this article was first written, I have added fifteen more years) and, during this period, I saw the TOEFL score being raised from 400 to 550. But I must confess that neither the academic standards of the institution of higher learning nor the quality of American students has improved noticeably, and in equal measurement to the rise in TOEFL score for non-American students.

Somehow we believe that if a foreign student cannot speak or write English as well as we Texans do (and we know how well Texans speak and write English; we have a prime example in the White House), then he/she is unfit to receive *our* excellent education. The truth of the matter, seldom realized by us, is that the average academic ability of students from Asian countries is about two grade levels above our American students in math and science. Computer literacy in Asia, Southeast Asia and India is the highest in the world. It makes us all proud that our government is the best in the world, that only we know what is the true democracy, that our language is the one the whole world needs to learn to speak, that our society is the most desirable, and we just don't like being called lazy or ignorant because we know we are the hardest working and the most intelligent people on the face of the earth. And educators (actually the educational testing agencies which make a bundle of money from servicing the likes of TOEFL) uphold the required test as if it is their sacred duty to do so, not realizing (or purposely oblivious to) the fact that no other country in the world has any parallel prerequisites for admitting foreign students into their educational institutions.

But, come to think of it, China was exactly like that only a few centuries ago. Early Jesuit missionaries to China had noticed that, in spite of their high level of accomplishment in virtually every field of science, the Chinese knew very little of the outside world. They believed that China was at the center of the earth, that all foreigners were ignorant barbarians who seemed never able to speak Chinese well—the language that was so graceful and full of nuances, a language that even a two-year-old Chinese girl could speak—that their Emperor and his throne were worthy of adoration and admiration of the whole world, that their gods would always be on their side and listen to the emperor's prayers. The Chinese were intelligent but proud and arrogant, well educated but ignorant of the world at large, righteous and self-respecting but discriminatory and biased when it comes to understanding and communicating with the people of other cultures. If all this sounds like I am a bit indignant, you are right, but only partially. I am trying to point out that these symptoms are very nigh identical with what is affecting—even ailing—the American mentality and "Texan attitude" in particular.

Around 1875, a Chinese boy came to apply for admission to an elite university on the U.S. east coast. The university officials denied him admission because he was only sixteen years old and from China, and he spoke English with a peculiar accent. Standing up to the officials, the boy declared, "It is you, who think that language fluency and age are the sole indicator of a person's intellect, who should be barred from the educational institution." (The boy later became one of the most renown statemen of the late Qing dynasty.) Now, more than a century later, the same mindset seems to exist in many of the U.S. education policymakers. And occasionally still, one sees on the rear of automobiles the signs that read:

[AMERICA, LOVE IT OR LEAVE IT], or

[DON'T MESS WITH TEXAS]

Then, perhaps I could whisper into your ears, that the Chinese once thought so, too, much more strongly, in fact, and so did the Romans and Greeks and Babylonians. That I am glad that you are now thinking about yourselves exactly the same way my ancestors had thought of themselves several centuries ago. It is sort of comforting to know that we are actually very much alike even in this regard. For, after all, the East is sometimes West, and the West is sometimes East, and you—that is, we Americans who are the most western of all Westerners—are now behaving quite like the Easterners once did, because we believe that America is the center of the world. We are proud, and we are smarter and more hardworking than all the others, and we are building our culture better and higher than any other in the world, almost as high as the Tower of Babel. All we need to heed is that the American language will not get confounded.

Meanwhile, congratulations! We Americans have finally arrived!

13

Skin, Speech, and the Social Caste

July is the anniversary month of my coming to the United States, some four decades ago. Even after so many years, I could still recall the fear and loneliness I felt the moment I stepped off the plane at Seattle airport. That feeling of desperation was suddenly shattered by a friendly voice calling my name, and I was rescued. The voice belonged to the sister-in-law of the American missionary (Doris Brougham) who had helped me so much in coming to America.

The station-wagon ride from the airport, the street scenes, then to the residence on the Seattle hillsides, the spacious and luxurious house with ceiling-high glass walls to look out to the magnificent forests below, the impeccably appointed room with an adjacent bathroom that was so clean that you could "eat off the floor," the credibly soft bed that I feared for a second that I was going to *sink through*, and the first-ever "bacon-scrambled-egg-and-pancake and orange-juice" breakfast; these are the memories that are inexplicably still so fresh and vivid.

Now, after more than four decades, I actually feel more at home here in the United States than when I am back in Taiwan. Perhaps language has something to do with it. Nearly all my Chinese friends and even my wife say my Chinese sounds more like American missionaries trying to speak Chinese, meaning that the inflections in my spoken Chinese are awkward, confusing and often downright wrong. And my wife tells me that when I talk in my dreams, I only speak in English. I suppose this is excusable, since Chinese was my third language. To make the matter worse, every day for the past thirty-five years, English has been not only the language I use exclusively in my teaching but at home also, with my American-born children. In fact, I sometimes forget that I am NOT a native-born American.

But you can be sure that, for many years, I was keenly aware of the fact that "this land is NOT my land," and that I had a distinct feeling that I was not an equal among the people of this land. This feeling was particularly strong during the first few years when I was studying in a university in a southern state, and I often felt unsure how I ought to fit in with the surroundings. I still remember the perplexed feeling in seeing the [COLORED ONLY] and [WHITES ONLY] signs posted on the rest rooms at bus terminals, and felt obligated to count the number of seat rows on the city bus in order to sit exactly halfway down the isle, thus making sure that I was not invading into either the [COLORED ONLY] or the [WHITES ONLY] territory. For, I reasoned, I could only classified myself as the [MEDIUM-DONE], not as pale and *rare* as the [WHITES] or as dark and *well-done* as the [COLORED].

The first U.S. college I attended was (then) fiercely segregational, and there were times I felt uncomfortable among the all lily-whites. I did reason that, after all, I have been admitted to this institution and, therefore, I must have been classified NOT as a colored person. But each time I looked at my own complexion with this natural, built-in tan, I wondered if the admissions office might have been somewhat color-blind. And there were times I had this urge to tell my roommates the first ethnic joke I heard back in Taiwan.

The story goes that, when God was creating mankind, he put a batch of clay figures into the heavenly oven and, after a while, took the tray out, only to find that it was over-baked, DARK. So he put this batch in Africa. He put another batch in, only to have it out a bit too soon, soft and PALE, and he put it up north from Africa, into what was later known as Europe. This time he was more careful, since he had only enough dough left for one last batch. This time it came out just right, good and perfect LIGHT BROWN. And he put these well-baked figures in the land of Cathay (that is, China), in the fertile plains between the highest mountain ranges and the largest ocean.

I am sure you won't have any trouble figuring out who made up this silly joke. But I didn't dare tell this joke to any of my friends on campus. For the school was founded on fiercely religious—some would call it "fundamental"—persuasions, and I was not about to risk my educational opportunity because of some silly joke, since I had begun to find out that they all seemed to have an awfully sensitive mind when it came to the matter of God and man, and any indiscrete joke may be regarded as sacrilegious.

During my second year there, one student from Ethiopia was admitted to the university. He was a short man, easy to smile and of very friendly demeanor. He had sharp facial features, and his skin color was VERY dark. Soon some talk began circulating among students, for I overheard my roommates and their friends—all theology majors—saying that this person was admitted because he was not the "regular" colored person which, I assumed to mean he was not one of the black people of the United States. Well, it so turned out that the matter was not as simple socially and *spiritually* straightforward as the college administration and students had assumed.

During the "Spiritual Conference" that semester, a concern was brought to the attention of the college Board of Trustees that many *spiritual* guests attending the conference were disturbed by the presence of this single dark-skinned face among the body of three thousand plus lily-white students. (There were actually a sprinkle of browns: about a dozen or more Asian students, several from Hawaii (American citizens, of course); a handful from Korea; one young lady born in Okinawa but was adopted by an American couple and, hence, assumed their surname Arthur; and three Chinese, one each from the Mainland, Hong Kong, and Taiwan.)

So, one day, toward the end of the Spiritual Conference, the administration—actually it was no less than the President of the University himself—took the pulpit one morning, and offered an official stance and a *biblical* justification to the entire student body and, more importantly, the participants in the spiritual meetings. The admission of this student was biblically based, the president pronounced with an air of authority, because he was from Ethiopia. For, after all, Philip the Disciple of the Lord did preach to an Ethiopian eunuch (*cf.* The *Book of Acts* of the Apostles), and Ethiopian Christians were the fruits of the very missionary work of Disciple Philip. Therefore, it was an *evangelical obligation* of the university *to admit him even if he was colored.* Besides, this theology student would be returning to Ethiopia after completing his *education here*, to bring the Gospel to his *native countrymen over there*, and *not to remain here* in the United States.

That same evening, this Ethiopian student marched through various buildings on the campus including the library where I was studying that night, wearing the full and colorful native costume of Ethiopia. Even without uttering a word, his intention behind the demonstration walk through the campus buildings was all too clear. And the very next day, this Ethiopian student left this evangelical campus, never to return again. In thinking back to this incident, I had wondered many times what this Ethiopian theology student would have told his native friends, his relatives, and fellow Christians, about the belief and practice of this university which prided itself as being *evangelical* Christian in words and deeds, about the mindset of American Christians, and about the leadership of the university which promoted the school to be the guardian and defender of Biblical truths, the West Point of Christian orthodoxy.

After graduating from that university, I did further graduate studies at Chicago Conservatory, and became involved in the music ministry of a Japanese congregation in Chicago's Northshore area. There I became acquainted with a gracious lady who was active not only in the church but also in the Chicago-area Japanese communities. I learned that she lived with her daughter and son-in-law in a nice house in the Northshore suburb, a rather exclusive residential district. Although the house was bought and paid for by this widowed lady, the legal paper showed that her son-in-law, an American, had paid for and thus owned the house. Either the ordinance or the unwritten code observed and put into practice by the real estate agencies had prevented any non-whites from owning a house in that exclusively [WHITES ONLY] residential district. I recalled another example of the kind: long before World War II, signs were posted around the "Europeans-and-Americans-only" residential district in Shanghai, China, that read:

[CHINESE AND DOGS NOT ADMITTED]

During these years, I often heard a phrase from some Christians who practiced segregation: "Equal but separate." The odd thing about this is that these God-fearing people truly believed this to be a biblical statement. This was the phrase quoted and preached on by the president of that university in South Carolina that I attended, and by a few living in Chicago's Northshore suburb who were members of the same church where the Japanese congregation held their Sunday services. The Japanese services were held in the afternoon, well after the white congregation finished their morning services and cleared the premises.

"Equal but separate" was a perspective of social class, a softer version of social caste system, that posed a challenge on my attempt to comprehend the working of the attitude and mindset of the American society. For this was something I had never thought of, or had any need to think about, in the past, since I had never observed such social practice in the Far East. This is not to say that ethnic biases and social castes and ranks of men and women did not exist in the Far East. In Taiwan, for example, there were biases between the native Taiwanese and the Mainlanders, or between the Chinese and the Aborigine people. Even today, the national and cultural biases between the native Japanese and those new Japanese transplanted from Korea or Taiwan are still detectable. Rather, what I am referring to is that such biases were seldom, if ever, articulated and put in documented laws or ordinances, or as a theological *manifesto*. And to see this practiced in the land of the free, by the people who pride themselves as being the most democratic and open-minded in the world?!

But, perhaps such were the things of the past, many decades ago. We are now all proud that America has certainly come a long way from segregation days, that we the people have overcome much of the ethnic prejudices and social injustices. We certainly have come a long way, and we even have resolved, at least to a tangible extent, the newer social issues such as women and gay people serving in the armed forces and holding clerical positions. We have done away with much of the so-called political incorrectness, and we have become accustomed to address letters with "Dear Sir/Madam," "Dear Mr./Ms," and the indiscriminating "his/her" and "he/she." And theologians are reluctant to say if God is HE, SHE, or IT. It has even become a social uncertainty if a father can take a bath with his own toddler daughter, or a mother with her young son. Teachers are prohibited from posting students' grades, so mandated by the privacy act, because Johnnie's mother doesn't want any psychological trauma to her son in knowing that his schoolwork is not as good as that of his class mates. So the school administration advocates social promotion; every student regardless of proficiency and academic skills achievement would be promoted to the next grade level since the administrators do not want a parent group to make any connection between grades and ethnic and social classes, or between the psychological and behavioral symptoms.

After all, this United States of America is the most democratic society, where everyone and every opinion must be regarded as correct or at least deserving a hearing. And, so, everyone with any opinion is busy shouting at the top of his/her voice above all the hollering, all wanting to be heard. And I sincerely doubt if anyone can really hear what he/she is saying.

I begin to feel rather dizzy about all this social and political correctness and incorrectness, about newer and ever more probing codes of ethics. And in times like this, I remember what Abraham Lincoln had said, that "[true] democracy is where everyone is right when everyone is wrong." I know, too, that Mr. Common Sense and Ms. Mutual Respect have stopped speaking quite some time ago, in the face of all the shouting matches, both of them having been declared to be no longer "politically correct." For the clamor is truly deafening.

What price social equity, and what price political correctness?

14

Man, Woman, and the Social Caste

Recently I took my children to visit a lady at Good Samaritan Village in Denton. For many years, Betty Bailey had been very active in our church; she was a soprano in the choir, and she and her husband Joe Bailey were the church historians. (Joe and I were colleagues; he was a librarian at the university.) A few months after Joe passed away, Betty moved to an apartment in the Village, and I provided transportation to the church whenever she was able to come to choir rehearsal. Some time later, her attendance at the church became more and more infrequent.

This time, my children and I went to her apartment unannounced, but she recognized me immediately, and we had a very pleasant visit that lasted nearly an hour. Toward the end, we invited her to the Village chapel and, there, we engaged in a little music making: my children sang while I played the piano, and my daughter played a few simple clarinet pieces. Shortly after we began making music, another lady—also a resident of the Village—came into the chapel, sat down and listened to our little impromptu recital and, afterward, joined in our conversation. In saying good-bye, they invited us to come back as often as we possibly could.

On our way home, my daughter Jocelyn, then thirteen years old, asked a rather observant question: "Daddy, why are there so many ladies and only a few men in the Village?" I thought for a moment and offered my simplistic answer: "Because, on the average, woman lives longer than man." "Why, I didn't know that!" "Well, it is because nature has made it so."

I doubt if Jocelyn had any comprehension of the significance of my short answer. But it is true, I believe, that the all-wise nature had made it so, for good reasons. Contrary to the generally held view, or at least to what is implied in the common saying, that woman is a "weaker sex" and, therefore, by implication, male is a stronger sex, the female gender has been equipped with faculties that are superior to those of the male gender, that these faculties enable them to not only prolong their life span longer than man's but, more importantly, also allow them to more effectively protect and preserve the life of the species. In contrast, the male gender is outwardly more physical and strong, but less fit for survival. Males are by nature more direct and aggressive. They are more territorial minded and therefore are seen to be more protective of their "possessions." (See how the male elephant seals protect and fight for their harem of females.) But they are less shrewd and subtle, less accommodating and yielding. And, in their single-minded pursuit to fulfill their natural urges, they become impulsive and foolhardy. In short, males are exhibitionistic and egotistical, easily given to self-aggrandizement even at a great cost, seldom able to see beyond their upward pointed nose. But, before many of my own gender decry foul against the above assessment of male *versus* female characterization, perhaps I should give a brief narrative on how I have come to such awareness.

It all started when I was about ten years old when, on one Christmas, my parents gave me a book for a present. I remember that I was quite disappointed in not getting my usual gifts, guns and swords, that every Japanese boy wanted in those wartime years. So, in disgust I put the book away, and it was quite a while afterward Christmas that I picked up the book to read. Once I began reading, however, I found it difficult to put it down until I finished reading the entire book.

The book was about the life and experience of a dragonfly, narrated from the perspective of a human (the author) who dreamed one day that he became a dragonfly, and thus the adventure began. The world and life from the dragonfly's point of view was totally fascinating to a young mind, and the book aroused in me an intense interest and curiosity in natural science. Later, I entered college with an intention to become a biologist; instead, I graduated with a degree in agricultural economics, as it was the wish of my parents. Still, that interest in living creatures continued and remained with me until this day.

It was during the college years also that I began to take interest in the difference between female and male creatures. No, I am not referring to the obvious. What I am referring to is the difference in the kind and degree of faculties, both physical and mental, that nature has endowed in the male and female genders, and the difference in the way the male and female engage these faculties in maintaining their positions in their species and in securing the survival of the life of individual creatures as well as that of the species. And the most fundamental and undergirding reason for the existence of such differences is the greatest of concerns of all living things: the preservation of the species.

I found, to my amazement, that males are rather inept when it comes to the preservation of the species, that the only truly significant role they play is that of procreation. However, there, too, the behavior of the males is often haphazard. They are selfish, arrogant, physically more prominent, in general, but have less acute senses and a rather dull mental perception. And they are quite dispensable in terms of the survival of the species. As a member of this male gender, such a realization was rather humbling. But it is quite clear that all-wise nature has made it so, and there is ample evidence to this in nature. A few cases in point:

We know how useful male bees are; very little, except for one particular *functional* occasion. And, under severely adverse conditions, their worker bees (all female) would not hesitate to systematically eliminate the excesses of these almost-good-for-nothing males. Take male lions, the king of all beasts. In actuality, however, they are a pitiful lot. When their prime is past and the vital male-usefulness spent, they often are expelled from the pack. They wander alone and, being too weak or too slow to hunt, they scavenge to barely survive. At the end, they die of starvation, long before the full tenure of their potential life span.

Or, we may draw a more dramatic—and perhaps a little sadly comical—example from the spider and mantis.

The female of certain species of spider (known as "black widow") and of the "praying" mantis would kill and consume their "partners in action" right during the course of mating. Of course these male spiders and mantes are in no way intimidated by such a doomed prospect; males are males, no matter what. And in fulfilling their destined role, male mantes, even with their heads bitten off or half of their torsos gone (into the stomach of the mating females), will continue to perform, their body maintaining a few more *involuntary spasms*, in order to complete the ultimate and definitive performance of their lives.

Man calls this creature *mantis*; the Latin root word *mantis* meaning "prophet, diviner," is an allusion to the creature's raised front legs as if in a posture of praying. (Hence, the adjective *praying* before mantis—thus "*praying* praying [creature]"—is redundant. Also, *necromancy* is somewhat related to mantis: *necro* is from *nek*—to kill—and *mancy* is derivative of *mantis*, divination, soothsayer, *praying* prophet, even *mad*.) It is somewhat *sad* and *mad* (meaning crazy) that nature has endowed the male gender with this all-consuming urge to "perform" but not much else. It is sadder and madder still that males—and human males in particular—regard this urge as often the sole means of self-gratification and self-aggrandizement.

An ancient Japanese folk tale offers a very eloquent explanation, humorous and mischievous but quite true:

When the creation of heaven and earth was completed, god summoned all the creatures to come before his presence. The first twelve creatures that arrived at the heavenly court were given the honor of dominion over the districts of the creation after their names. The zodiac thus established, god turned his attention to the matter of procreation of the creatures to whom he had given life, and he began to dictate the frequency of procreative activity for each of the creatures. To one creature, god would say, "Thou shalt *go into* once a month," and to another "Thou shall *lie together* twice a year," and so on and so forth. Every creature accepted the ordained lot obediently, and retreated from god's presence with a silent prostration.

Then stepped forth the haughty Mr. Horse. "What shall my lot be, Lord?" Mr. Horse inquired loudly, obviously wanting all the creatures to hear god's pronouncement for him while displaying his mighty instrument.

Peeking over the thick heavenly chronicle, god announced:

"THOU SHALT LIE DOWN **ONCE EVERY TWO YEARS.**"

"There must be some mistake!" protested Mr. Horse, shaking his long head furiously and breathing heavily through his long snout:

"How could it be, seeing that YOU have given me such a magnificent tool?
It would be a cruel limitation!"

Mr. Horse bickered long and badgered hard with god. Finally, the exasperated god lost all his *transcendental cool*:

"GET THEE BEHIND, YOU HORSE-HEAD BEAST!" he thundered; "FOR I HAVE SPOKEN!"

While the holy wrath was still reverberating between heaven and earth, a timid and pale-skinned creature stepped forward. Walking awkwardly on his two skinny hind legs, he bowed low before god.

"What shalt my lot be? Do command, my Lord, and I shall obey,"

entreated this little creature, fearing all the while that god, still in his all-righteous wrath, might deny him altogether.

Then, behind the thundering dark clouds and lightning flashes, came the loud voice, re-echoing throughout the whole creation:

"W-H-O C-A-R-E-S!!!!!!"

> ("***KAT-TE NI SHIYAGARE!***" in Japanese, literally means
> "DO **WHATEVER YOU PLEASE!**"
> Note also: the six exclamation marks signify
> the "perfect" will of god.)

WHO CARES, ***indeed!*** And this little, pitifully looking creature who walks on his two hind legs has been indulging in his unregulated, licentious activity of the chamber (or out of chamber) ever since.

But we are human, and not animals, and we are wiser. And we have learned, in a continuous process of learning, how to coexist as equal partners. Social, ethical and gender discriminations are a thing of the past. After all, we are homo-*sapiens* or even homo-*sapiens-sapiens*, meaning, of course, we are wiser and wisely-wiser than other creatures. Still, from time to time we are made to admit that we are not really much nobler and wiser than other creatures, that our primitive instinct and the male ego in particular are still rampant. And when in those rare moments of self-congratulation that we have become superior beings or attained a superior status in life, we are suddenly brought back to a rude realization, as Sigmund Freud would lament, that we still retain much of the primitive urge. And Freud could have added that *that* raw and rude urge is more observable in the male gender.

Some years after World War II and the Korea War, a survey was conducted, I have been told, on the reasons why so many American service men chose to take Asian women as their wives, instead of the more physically attractive and culturally familiar American women. The two top reasons that those surveyed gave are rather enlightening. One was that Asian women hold their age much better, meaning they don't seem to wither and wrinkle as easily; the second was that Asian women are more submissive and more willing to help—or, serve—their husbands.

Are they truly more subservient? Well, let me share with you that it is here where the true mystery and wisdom of Oriental women can be discovered. Oriental women realize and accept the fact that males will always be "males," that even when they are full-grown, they remain immature and still a spoiled brat at heart. Their ego is easily bloated by a few flattering words, a little promotion in social status, and this same ego is equally fragile, easily punctured. They would quickly turn their wrath on their spouses and even their children, as though it is all their fault. Of course, you remember what Adam said when he and Eve were caught eating the forbidden fruit: "*She did* it *first!*"

But the wisdom of Asian women also recognizes that longevity of life and usefulness of their men is not unchangeable; it is very much in their (female) hands, that it can be determined by how they (the male) are treated. So, wise Asian women continue to behave humbly and submissively, to keep relatively quiet in the company of their men's friends, and even so willingly to walk a few steps behind their men (thus to be more free and not be seen to giggle and exchange glances or a word or two among themselves while their men walk haughtily ahead). They, the female, know too that being confrontational and combative with their born-brute companion is actually futile and ineffective in controlling them and keeping them in check. They know too well, too, that each needs the other for procreation and preservation of their species. And since the male gender is short in wisdom to see by themselves the need to change their own foolhardy ways, or short on capacity to do so, it is the nature-entrusted responsibility of the female to accommodate and support their worse half, to make them functional a bit longer and, at the same time, to maintain harmony in life and sustain its continuity.

What price and what value is social class? Things are not always what they seem. And the Oriental women know the true power of their slender hands that rock the cradle, as well as the power of their pillow talk when the night falls and their men are bare and defenseless. Oriental women know that they must continue to behave humbly and submissively. After all, it is they who are meek and lowly who will ultimately inherit the earth by outliving their men.

And I hear the voices of a treble chorus resounding from the four corners of the earth with joyous shouts:

"Banzai, Ban-banzai!!!"

"Wanswei, Wan-wan-swei!!!

"Long Live Asian Women!!!"

15

Man, Woman, and the Social Caste (Conclusion)

The social life of my family is decidedly limited, and our circles of friends are of three categories: fellow professors at the university where I teach; colleagues of my wife at the (Japanese) company where she works; and the choir members of the church where I was also the minister of music. Until several years ago, my wife used to love inviting large company of guests but, now, with a full-time position in the computer-industrial sector, planning and cooking up a full menu of dinner became impossibly difficult. In recent years we have resorted to inviting friends for *pot-luck* supper, finding it a decidedly more convenient and happy compromise. On these occasions, we often would include a few international students on the guest list, especially the music students from Asia, thereby providing an attractive after-the-dinner musical variety show. And on many occasions we were even successful in prompting the dinner guests to join in the merrymaking.

A few years ago, we invited a Japanese couple among the dinner guests. The husband was a medical doctor and research scientist visiting Southwestern Medical School in Dallas, and his wife had just arrived from Japan to be with him for a couple of months before he concluded his work in the United States. While the doctor spoke fluent English, his wife had virtually no knowledge of English. And since I was the only one in the company that evening who could also speak Japanese, I became the instant interpreter for her in the conversation with the other guests, especially when her doctor husband was preoccupied with the American university professor guests. And the conversation turned to the subject of *Western* husband *versus American* husband. I think it all started when my wife casually mentioned that since she was usually late in coming home most of the work days, I had gradually assumed the daily chore of preparing the evening meals, so that our children would have their supper at a more regular hour, and that my cooking had become rather respectable. "*Yee neh, urayamashii wah! Watashi no hito wa son-na koto zen-zen desu yo!*" exclaimed the Japanese lady. I had to translate it *verbatim* to the other guests: "she said, 'Oh, how wonderful! I am jealous. My man could never do anything like that!'" All eyes were on the doctor professor, and we all laughed. Grinning somewhat sheepishly, he offered an explanation worthy of a true Japanese man: "*Samurai wa dai-dokoro he hai-razu*" ("A *samurai* [*i.e.*, a true Japanese man] would never [con-]descend to *dai-dokoro* [kitchen]!" And we all burst out in roaring laughter.

Japanese men refer to their wives as "*ka-nai*" and the Chinese as "*nei-ren.*" *Kanai* means "[the person] inside the house," while *neiren* has a parallel connotation of "the inside person." Clearly, it signifies the traditional societal notion of the proper place for wives. Even today when many Asian wives have their own careers in the "outside" world, these same terms are in continuous use and no feminist group ever decries foul. And, as both the doctor and his wife began to explain to the rest of us, perhaps in a light-hearted way, what he or she does or does not do in the house, I began to realize for the first time that there is a deeper significance in the referential title "inside the house" for Asian wives.

She complained, even with a smile lingering on her face, that she was the one to seek out teachers and make arrangements for their children's dance and piano lessons, while he couldn't even remember the names of his own children. She also was the one to keep check on how their children did in school, and they in turn would come to their mother for any problems they had, in school or with their friends. And she "complained" that he didn't seem much interested in their children, casting an occasional glance at her man while she spoke.

At this point he chimed in. Looking at his wife, he said, "It is because I put all my trust in you, and I never doubted your decisions. You may think I have a bigger responsibility in our family's life, but in fact you make all the life decisions, and all I do is work outside the house. You are the inner strength, the pillar of our family!" To which she smiled broadly, and whispered to me, "*Sonna koto itte, johdan bakkari!*" ("So he said; it's all a joke!") And as I looked at her, I could see that she was actually not altogether discontent with the share of her role in the life of their family. And I realized, too, that my supper chore is a privilege, an opportunity entrusted to me to play a vital part in the upbringing of our children. And I do the chore not because I have to, or as duty required but, rather, I am able to contribute.

Indeed, Asian wives have been seen by the Westerners as the model of domestic (or domesticated) submissiveness. But one would only need to read the book of Proverbs to recognize how "Oriental" are all the descriptions of the quality of a virtuous wife. Besides being submissive, Asian wives are expected to be "*diligent, energetic* and *hard working*" and they "*watch for bargains,*" and how! It is educational, almost inspirational, to watch how Chinese and Jewish housewives would barter tirelessly for every item of purchase in the market. These virtuous qualities of Asian wives are in fact rather *biblical* (these same adjectives in quotation marks in *italics* in the preceding sentences are used in the last chapter, *e.g.*, verse 17, of the Book of *Proverbs* in the Old Testament to describe virtuous wives). In turn, Asian (that is, Oriental) husbands are always proud of the virtuosity of their wives, and would be quick to let their peers know about it.

The interesting thing about all this is that Asian husbands would hesitate to praise the beauty of their wives, and we also may note that the beauty of a wife is never extolled in the Bible. In fact, the unwritten virtue of Asian wives is that their appearance is to be homely or, at least, to be concealed. Beauty concealed is a sign of humility and, if anything is worthy of revealing, it should be their *inner beauty*. Asian wives dress rather modestly, they walk quietly and humbly behind their men. And I have wondered how many Westerners have ever attempted to appreciate the significance of the hump of a big bow tied at the back of Japanese women's traditional gowns (*kimono*, literally means "wear-thing'). The true function of this hump is to *de-emphasize* the curvature of the hip's profile, thus to make the whole back seem "bent" as if in humble bowing. And the same wide-band *obi* (belt) is tied tight and *chest high* at the front, as if—there again—to suppress and de-emphasize the protruding breast-line. In a sense, the entire dress "code" is to make women less appealing (to other men); such is the same function of Arabic (Muslim) women's *yashmak* (face veil).

While modesty is considered a female virtue in both the East and West, it may refer to quite different things. I still remember the remark of an American missionary friend by the name of Roy Habecker, who grew up in a predominantly Mennonite community in Washington Boro, Pennsylvania. He told me how shocked he was to see a young mother sitting across from him on the train, baring her breast to feed her infant baby. While Western wives would never think of breastfeeding infants in public places, such a sight is still not uncommon in the

Far East and Southeast Asia. But, alas, like beauty, virtue is also very much in the eyes of the mind of the beholder.

Once, the famous British explorer-Orientalist Sir Richard Francis Burton was traveling with a caravan in the Arabian dessert, when he witnessed an incident: A Muslim woman fell from the camel, head first. Landing on her head with limbs all sprawled, her robe fell over her head, thus uncovering her legs and thighs up in the air. Thereupon, her husband raised his hands and face and loudly praised Allah, because his wife was able to *maintain her modesty wholly unblemished*. Even in the fall that bared her legs, this virtuous wife of his had managed to keep her *yashmak* securely in place over her face.

Following the end of World War II, there were dramatic changes in Asian women's appearance, from make-up to dresses to shoes. No longer were restrictions and codes of ethics either regulated or imposed by the tradition especially during those difficult war years, and women of nearly every age group had Hollywood movies to emulate and inspire them to instantaneously become Western. When Audrey Hepburn's *Roman Holidays* came to Asia, it looked as if the entire hairdressing industry had to learn overnight to cope with the demand of epidemic proportion of cutting women's forehead hair short. And farm girls who had seldom worn shoes of any kind, and had wide and thick feet with outwardly spread toes, were now trying to squeeze into slender and pointed high-heel shoes, and to learn to walk even awkwardly, knees half bent, just to keep from falling down. To many tradition-minded Asian men, those new sights were not only bad-taste, but also were outright immoral.

One Sunday, in our Hualien Presbyterian Church, Mr. Wei, an attorney and revered—even feared—*head* elder of the church, took the pulpit. With the Bible held high in his right hand, he denounced the new and wholly UN-Christian-like appearance of many women in the church without naming names. He cited verses from the Old Testament in which women's long hair is praised, and from the New Testament the Apostle Paul's admonition to women to "humble themselves before men." "To humble" means to lower oneself, and not to elevate, and wearing high heels to make them stand taller (than men) is tantamount to "elevating oneself" above men and therefore is a demonstration of pride and arrogance." The sermon was powerful and fiery, with a ringing of righteous indignation and divine wrath.

That was when Elder Wei's own daughter was still in elementary school. A few years later, his daughter was all "teen-ager" and all "Western," and we suspected that *Mrs.* Wei had some say on how their daughter should dress in step with the fashion trend. Since then, we had never again heard of Mr. Wei's sermon on women's hairdos, makeup and highheel shoes again.

Like our Japanese medical doctor and the revered Elder Wei, Asian men may boast how masterly they are, that their wives and children walk humbly and obediently behind them, along the straight and narrow path. But don't ever think that Asian women and Asian wives are all that meek and without any authority. They are in fact the virtual rulers in their domestic life and, as the Japanese doctor had so eloquently insinuated, "the inner strength and the pillar" of their homes.

Outwardly meek and submissive, all Asian mothers yield a considerable authority and, with it, are very protective of and totally devoted to the welfare of their children. To Western eyes, it may even appear that Asian mothers are overly possessive, overly protective, overly competitive, and overly devoted to their children, at times even to the detriment of (the mother's) own well-being. At the same time, I wonder whether Western mothers could ever appreciate the extent of joy and satisfaction these Asian mothers draw from their children's achievements, not the sort in being on a football team, cheer-leading brigade or homecoming queen, but something of a more lasting value, the fruition of dedication to work and study.

Asian mothers are notorious in pressuring their children to succeed, to do no less than their utmost best. They rejoice with their children in their successes, and endure with their children in their setbacks and failures. American mothers may raise eyebrows in hearing that Asian mothers would chide their children in getting "only 89 points" on the test, and prod them to do better the next time, not realizing that it is their way of encouraging their children never to be complacent, to make them realize that, even with their best effort, there may still be room for improvement. And, throughout their entire life, Asian mothers remain devoted and proud of their children, whether they succeed gloriously or fall short of the parents' expectation.

This protective instinct of Asian mothers will go so far as to make them endure what may appear to Westerners as a painful shame. Even in this modern world, it is not uncommon (and often overlooked or tolerated) that Asian men—especially those who are socially successful but even those who are not at all distinguished—have mistresses. Perhaps astonishing or immoral to Western "Victorian" morality is the fact that polygamy, in the form of a "common-law wife," is an accepted, if not publicly recognized, societal practice. And these "secondary counsel" wives occasionally are seen to live rather harmoniously within the same household, with the *principal* wife being duly referred to as *Jieh-Jieh* (Elder Sister) or *Dah-Jieh* (the *Big* or *Eldest* sister) by the other *Joannies-come-lately*. There, the principal (the *legally* recognized) wife has the near-absolute authority over the entire family affairs, and yields her power even on the line-up of not only the "affairs of the chamber" but also of all the children of wives of various ranks.

In the bygone eras when betrothals were arranged by family elders long before the youths became of age, sometimes while they were yet infants or toddlers, marriage was a matter of family duty. Hence, "*What does love got to do with marriage?!*" In facing the harsh reality of survival, one of the most important concerns of the parent of a young marrying age woman was to give her a life from want, with a measure of assurance of a comfortable life. We can easily understand, therefore, why Reb Tevye (in the movie *Fiddler on the Roof*) was so quick and ready to agree with his young daughter Tzeitel to wed the village butcher Reb Lazar "Wolf" who was *so old*—even older than Tevye—*but wealthy*. Besides, the primary and the shared duty of the wives, therefore, was to maintain the welfare of the household, maintain peace and harmony among all members of the extended family, and, above all, to sustain and uphold the honorable name of the ancestral lineage. Hence, the position of the children in the order of the family, as well as the education and the future career engagement of the children, become a matter of primary importance and shared responsibility, far, far greater than the little concern of female jealousy over who is the principal wife and who is the secondary counsel.

In the days when the whole country was in continuous turmoil, suffering from wars with foreign invasions, devastated by local hoodlums and roaming bandits, famines and other natural and manmade disasters, the poor starved and died in the fields by countless thousands. Tales abound from the China of old about children selling themselves to slavery so to have money to bury their parents, or parents selling their children in order to have money to buy food to sustain the life of the remaining ones. There, the line between the ethical and moral codes, family honor and struggle for survival, becomes all but indistinguishable. Hence, life's lot in becoming even a secondary or tertiary counsel, or any place in a family with some assurance of life's sustenance, was all too sufficient a ground for gratitude to the heavenly spirits.

Hence, all the hopes and dreams of a mother were heaped upon the prospect of a good life for her children. Nothing, absolutely nothing else, is more important to a mother than her children's future. This was the underlying reason for a popular saying in China, "*Mu yi Zhi wei guei*" ("Mother's honor is measured by her child"). It is quite understandable, therefore, that Asian parents—and Asian *mothers* in particular—take so much pride in and often seem so *showoff*-ish of their children's accomplishments. Asian mothers just could not stop talking about the successes of their children, especially if their children are either medical doctors or lawyers. But there are also reasons of cultural and historical backdrops for this.

In the age-old caste system of Asia, opportunity to succeed in society was often predetermined by family lineage. This is particularly so in regard to government positions. And in the countries that had a long history of being another country's colony, the natives were regarded as "second-class" citizens. Any future prospect of a child attaining a position in government office was nothing more than a *mirage*. Under the fifty-year Japanese rule, for example, virtually no Taiwanese were ever admitted to political science or engineering majors in the university. Thus, in those colonial years, the best future career opportunity for the brightest and most promising students was in the practice of medicine or law.

This political-societal environment created ranks of doctors and attorneys in Taiwan who were also in the family lineage of doctors and lawyers. In Taiwan as well as Korea, the other colony of Japan before the end of the War, this caste of doctor-lawyer families has become a unique societal phenomenon, such that no young doctor or lawyer would ever (be allowed by his family to) take as his wife a young lady who is not from the family of doctor-lawyer, or a daughter of a doctor-lawyer family would take a young man for a husband who is not a graduate of a medical or law school. This is the Taiwanese—actually, a Pan-Asian—brand of "*Blest be the TIE that binds.*" And the proud Asian mothers would never cease to refer to their children as "my DOCTOR son" and would want the whole world to know.

I have been told that this is also true of Jewish mothers. (Jews are Asians, too, in case you didn't know. Hence the term "Oriental Jews.") The Jews were, for a long time, also an oppressed and colonized people, as Chinese, Taiwanese, and Koreans were. Until after World War II, few full-blooded Jews held high government positions in the United States or in European countries. Hence the explanation for the phenomenon of Jewish doctors and lawyers aplenty. (Somewhat parallel to this is the phenomenon of so many Jewish musicians and bankers, the professional arena where, as to be expected, now Asians are competing with Jews.) My Jewish friends have shared with me how their mothers prodded them ceaselessly, incessantly over the years, to succeed. I had two good Jewish friends, one a classmate at Northwestern University by the name of Mark Pollack, and a colleague by the name of Melvin Solomon. Both were as toweringly tall as King Solomon (so I imagined, from the description in the Bible), as quick witted and extremely brilliant. And Mel once told me how his mother used to scold him every time he brought school papers home that did not have the perfect 100 score mark.

A Jewish family was enjoying a family outing on the beach when, suddenly, the mother was horrified to see that her son was in trouble a good distance from the shore. "Help!" the mother shrieked hysterically, waving both hands and pointing to the head wobbling in the waves. "Help! Help! My MEDICAL DOCTOR son is drowning!!!"

16

Monkey's Grip, Man's Grasp

The first semester in the United States was difficult for this Taiwanese, not sufficiently proficient in English, without sufficient financial support, and without any close friend with whom to share the feeling of loneliness. My parents sent me money just enough to pay for the first semester tuition and, to make the money last a bit longer, the university awarded me a work-loan "scholarship." I was assigned a job in the university's Art Gallery and Museum, well known in the region for its collection of religious art works by the Medieval and Renaissance European artists. I was often given the assignment to repair the old picture frames, and also to clean the workroom tables and sweep the floors at the end of each working day. Mr. Murry Havens, the bespeckled curator of painting and the Director of the Art Gallery, was straight talking but sincere and considerate, and seemed very satisfied with my work. He also asked me to use deodorant every day, so that my body sweating from hard work would not *doubly* trouble the Museum visitors in seeing this lone Asian working in the beautifully appointed artistic surroundings.

Then came the first Christmas vacation in the United States, but I did not have any place to go, since the whole campus was to be closed, and I would be shut out of the dormitory. A few days before the holiday began, Paul Habecker, one of my roommates, asked me if I would want to go home with him if I didn't have any other plans for the holiday. He was a cousin of Roy Habecker, the missionary friend I knew from the days I worked for the TEAM Gospel Radio (The Evangelical Alliance Mission), and had asked his parents if he could bring me home with him to Washington Boro, Pennsylvania. I was deeply moved and extremely grateful.

Pennsylvania winter was severe for this warm-blooded Taiwanese. But the days in the American home were warm and exceedingly comfortable. The pretzel-and-ice-cream snack after supper was incredibly delicious, and the glowing fireplace was like the scene I had only seen on Christmas cards from America. Paul's parents and grandparents (the Newcomers) were most hospitable, and Paul's elder sister Dotty (I think it was short for Dorothy) was particularly kind, and I felt as if I had been adopted into the Habecker family. I even went to the frozen river in the back of Paul's house, and learned to ice skate, played ice hockey with Paul, and got black and blue all over my arms and legs. I went with the family on outings, and visited Mennonite villages and marketplaces. The sight and sound of horse-drawn buggies was unforgettable. I was truly content, comforted, and filled with thankfulness.

My first Christmas Eve in the United States was spent in church with the Habeckers. The church on a hillside was small, the service was informal, and the people were down-to-earth, an old-fashioned rural community congregation. Even the Christmas program was somewhat *impromptu* and, as a part of special Christmas music, Paul was asked to play "O Holy Night" on his trumpet, and I was asked on the spot to sing. Although unprepared, I managed to muster enough courage to stand up for the first time in front of an American congregation, and I sang "*Go, Tell It On the Mountain*." After the service, I was warmly greeted and congratulated for my singing that was "the highlight" of the evening, so the kind-hearted people told me. Returning home and gathered around the fireplace, the family opened the Christmas presents, and I was most gratified to have a share: a *Bible Concordance* and a record set of Handel's *Messiah*. No doubt, *that* Christmas was the most unforgettable in my life.

A few weeks after coming back to the campus, Mr. Havens told me that I was let go of my work at the Museum. The news was a shock, but Mr. Havens was apologetic. I did not dare ask why, but only wondered if my work was not satisfactory, or if I had offended anyone in any way. On my way out of the Gallery, Mrs. Erma Havens, the Museum hostess and mother of Murry Havens, whispered to me that it was Dr. Bob, Jr.'s "instruction." Dr. Bob Jr. was the university president, a man with an imposing presence and an eloquent orator, a Shakespearean actor, and a connoisseur of fine arts, especially the painting and music of the classical period. In fact, the Art Gallery and Museum was his personal "project" and he often would come into the Gallery unannounced, to look around and to chat with the staff members. And he had seen me several times. I suspected that, for him, this lone Asian face did not fit well with all the saintly figures on the masters' paintings. (I learned that, a year or two after I left the university, Mr. Murry Havens had committed suicide.)

Toward the end of this second semester, I received a notice from the university business office, with a bill of about $280, and a note stating that the amount I owed the university must be paid in full before I could leave for the summer. That entire afternoon and well into the night, I could not think of anything else, wondering how I could ever come up with such a large amount of money. I knew too that I could never ask my parents for assistance. I don't recall I had ever prayed harder than that night at any other time in my life.

The very next morning, on my way to the dining hall, I stopped by the post office to check my mailbox, and found a letter from the Habecker family's little church in Washington Boro. Inside the envelope was a check in the amount of $300, a gift from the church. I stood there on the steps of the post office, transfixed, not able to believe what I was seeing in my hand. Right after breakfast, I went to the business office and paid the bill *in full*. With the rest of the money, less than twenty dollars, securely tucked into *my own* pocket, I felt *rich*. For even *before* I received the bill, I felt that God had already knew and had arranged to take care of my needs.

That was my own personal experience of "Crossing the Red Sea."

Graduating with a M.A. from a university in South Carolina, I spent one semester at the Chicago Conservatory (Roosevelt University), then another semester in post-graduate study at the University of Michigan (Ann Arbor). Exhausting the little savings I had, I returned to Chicago, and met Mr. and Mrs. Nakagawa at a Japanese church. Before World War II, they had owned and operated a Japanese elementary school in Seattle, but were rounded up with all the Japanese and held in the "concentration" camp until the end of the War. They then relocated to Chicago, and invested and managed three apartment buildings south of the Northshore area. At the Japanese church, I led music and the choir, and the Nakagawas (whose only child, a daughter, died before the War) took me in, offered me free room and board, and engaged me as their resident (that is, salaried) "fixed-it" man, to help with the never-ending repair chores in and around their apartments. I learned to fix broken glasses, change carpets, replace toilets, and resolve quarrels among the mostly Puerto Rican tenants. Once I found myself between two men fighting over a mistress, and lost all my wits when the younger one pulled out his pistol and pointed it barely an inch from my nose.

Later, while attending Southern Seminary in Louisville, Kentucky, there were periods of time when I could not afford three meals a day, and would have only one noon meal each day, drinking only water whenever I was hungry. But the "crossing the Red Sea" experience continued to sustain me. And with each difficult encounter, the recalling of the "Red Sea" experience helped to reinforce the belief that things will always work out, so long as I keep the faith, and remain truthful to myself. And I should pray only that, as Cardinal John Newman penned in his immortal hymn, *Lead, Kindly Light,* God will

> "Keep Thou my feet;
> I do not ask to see the distant scene—
> *One step enough for me.*"

Those experiences have also taught me a lesson in how to be steadfast with faith and maintain confidence in myself, no matter how adverse the circumstances may seem. I have learned that the first lesson in being happy in life is to be content and satisfied with oneself, with whatever possessions I have or do not have, and never envious of things beyond our personal bounds. And I have begun to understand why, more than anything else, God hated two things: pride (arrogance), and greed (envy). It may even be said that, in dramatic contrast to the early Greek (that is, Western) intellectual posture (*e.g.*, Aristotle's "great souled man" and the stoic sage's assertion of his own "moral independence from and equality with god" Zeus), the entire biblical (that is, Eastern) posture for man is to be humble, and to uplift the poor and the oppressed. The "sermons" that are repeated again and again throughout the Bible are that man should be without pride, and without greed.

But, oh, how difficult it is NOT to be proud. It is nearly impossible to be truly humble in spirit. And I sometimes think God has posed this absolutely impossible lesson on man. Put any two men together, and have them debate on any political, religious or any life issues, and you will quickly see that each person is trying to show that he knows more, and he is more right than the other. No one would like to admit that he is more "wrong" than the other man. Besides, at the very instance that a man claims that he has achieved humility, he has alreaddy lost the *true spirit of humility* in that very instant.

Then, perhaps there are important differences between a person having a sense of pride in him self, and a person who is arrogant, that which is referred to in the Bible as *haughtiness*. Through life experience, a man may begin to build confidence in his ability and judgment, a sense of right and wrong. Perhaps this is an "inner" pride or confidence in his ability to discern right from wrong. In contrast, haughtiness is an "outward" demeanor, condescending, regarding him self more superior than the others. But such differences are truly difficult to discern. How difficult is it for a man to be confident in his ability and judgment while truly respectful of others who do not agree with him?

Perhaps, then, it is easier to observe man's greed than man's pride. Greed makes a man want something beyond his need, something which is not rightfully his, something that belongs to another man. Greed is easily identifiable. If so, perhaps it is easier for man to control his greed. Or is it?

When our family evacuated to a small farming village to escape U.S. planes' bombing, a younger friend—my only friend in the village—taught me the art of survival; he showed me how to catch shrimp and crab in the mountain brooks with bare hands, and to crawl through the fence into the neighboring farmers' vegetable garden to steal cucumbers. Once he showed me where the farmers had placed bamboo traps in the river to catch larger shrimp. The basket traps were crudely made, but they were ingenious and effective. The opening was large enough but the bamboo blades with sharp end were pointed inside and the opening became gradually tapered toward a much smaller end, and there was bait—small pieces of fish—placed at the small end of the trap. The shrimp would go into the opening and even crawl through the basket to get to the bait. But, once inside, they would have a difficult time turning around and would find it impossible to go through the same passage, now with the sharp bamboo blade pointing at them.

Perhaps this crude farmer's bamboo trap is an eloquent picture of the trap of man, to entice a man lured by his own greed, not realizing that the cage of temptation is always easier getting in than getting out. And, once inside, there is little hope of escaping, for the greed is never satisfied. Instead, the greed becomes insatiable. Starting with a temptation of a little profit from manipulating bookkeeping, it emboldens a man when his act is not caught, and soon his act becomes cleverer, his heart becomes braver, and his greed becomes enormously enlarged. Today, stealing is no longer the desperate act of the poor, the lowly, and the hungry. Instead, we have the richest of our society robbing the poorer. Dennis Kozlowsky, Ken Lay, Joseph Nacchio, and many other millionaire CEOs have shown us how they have painted the true portraits of man's greed.

One Sunday shortly after the War (I was in my freshman year in high school), I accompanied my father to visit a Taiwanese aborigines church in the mountains near Hualien. Although it was a few years after the War ended, the tribal people continued to speak Japanese. My father preached in Japanese, and I sat with the villagers and sang hymns with them in Japanese. After the service, we enjoyed a "sumptuous" lunch with the village men, a genuine tribal meal that included a couple of meat dishes. There were wild beasts in the mountains, such as boar and wild dogs, and we were told that one of the meat dishes was monkey meat. My father and I were curious, since monkeys were the best tree climbers and would leap from tree to tree with great ease. Thereby the men volunteered their most ingenious way of catching monkeys.

"It is very simple," the men began. "You take a (dry-hardened) gourd, and make an opening at the small end, just large enough for a monkey to stick his hand in. Then you put peanuts in the gourd, and tie it tight to a tree. Then we wait for the monkey to come. The monkey smells the peanuts inside, peeks in but sees nothing in the dark. The monkey puts his hand through the small opening and grasps the nuts. That's when we approach the monkey. The monkey would scream and jump, trying to pull his hand out of the gourd to escape. But he could not. Because he *refuses to let go the nuts in his fist*. And we catch him!"

Impossible! I thought. How stupid could the monkey be? Would the monkey still hold on to the nuts when his life is threatened?

Ah, the greed of creatures. And it is a great irony of creation that, while man had passed far, far beyond the ape-stage on the evolution ladder, and while man regards himself as *sapien*, his wisdom and greed is not much different from that of the poor monkey who refuses to let go of the peanuts in his grip.

During my two years at Yuli Middle School (south of Hualien), I had three close buddies, Deng, Chang, and Yeh (surnames; I have forgotten their first names). We all lived close, on the same street going out from the town, and we would often wait for each other in the morning to go to school. The leader of our little group was Deng, tall, a year or two older than the rest, with a serious demeanor, strong and athletic. The rest of us were all comrades of equal standing: Chang had a complexion fairer than the rest of us, also athletic, and was very handsome; Yeh was also tall, with a round face and somewhat chubby (very well fed), and had an easy-going personality. Chang's family owned a large farm, and employed many servants. His mother was tall and pretty, and I heard that she was once his father's maid servant, but soon was taken to be the master's second wife because of her beauty.

The Yehs lived in a large house with an inner courtyard and many wings of rooms. The Yehs were rich, and the elder Yeh, already semi-retired and seldom ventured out of the house, had three wives, and my classmate's mother was the youngest—and prettiest—of the three. It was about three years after the War ended and, even in that small isolated rural town, people began getting used to wearing shoes, unless they were working in the muddy rice paddies. But I had noticed that Chang's and Yeh's mothers were always in their bare feet during the day. I was told that the elder Chang and the elder Yeh did not believe in shoes, regarding them as unnecessary luxurious items. Apparently, the more old-fashion-minded farmers, even the rich ones, believed that *healthy feet despised footwears.*

One day, coming home from school, I saw right across from our small parish residence a large crowd gathered in front of the Yeh mansion. The next day I learned that the elder Yeh had passed away during the night. I watched the funeral procession, with a large instrument band with *suona* (metal double-oboe that produced a shriekingly high-pitched noise) and drums playing the funeral dirge, followed by a long line of mourners, and learned that many of the loudly weeping and lament-chanting women were *hired mourners.* The greater number of mourners would indicate a higher standing of the deceased's social stature. And I saw my classmate in the funeral procession, walking among the sons and grandsons of the deceased, all wearing the burly sackcloth vest, white headband and black arm band. I also saw my classmate's mother, quietly sobbing, with white long cover over her head and face, and she was *wearing shoes.*

A few days after Elder Yeh died and my friend returned to school, I heard from my parents a most interesting story that had been told around the small town:

The elder Yeh was lying on his bed, now weak, feeble, and near death, and all his family members and servants stood surrounding his bed. Monks were chanting and reciting in the courtyard, and others quietly sobbings in the room. Occasionally, the elder Yeh would open his eyes and look around the room, gazing at his family whom he would soon leave behind. Then the mourning family saw Mr. Yeh raise his right arm, and make a gesture. His sons and wives bent over Mr. Yeh to inquire what was his last wish. Mr. Yeh, unable to speak, sighed audibly, and put out two fingers and waved, as if in denying. "What is it?" the anxious family asked. Again, the elder Yeh repeated the same gesture, feebly waving two right-hand fingers, and again sighed. This went on for a while, and no one seemed able to read the meaning of the gesture of Mr. Yeh's final instruction. Finally, someone noticed that Mr. Yeh's eyes were on the two candles dimly lit on the chest of drawers in a corner of the master's bedroom. Then, it all suddenly came to them. Mr. Yeh, with his last dying breath and strength, was trying to tell his family that burning *two candles in one room is a waste*.

We have read Charles Dickens' *A Christmas Carol*, and have seen it in various versions on the silver screen. And we always rejoice and sigh with glad relief at the redemptive deeds of Mr. Scrooge, and in shouting with Tiny Tim, the poor little crippled lad "Merry Christmas, and to every one, Good Night!" And we will all agree that there is an unmistakable lesson in Dickens' story, that "Greed is burden, and Generosity is its relief."

Recently (spring, 2007), an interesting case was brought to court in Washington, D.C. The lawsuit was for damage of property, brought by the plaintiff, an African-American, who was him self a business-law attorney. This well-to-do business lawyer accused a Korean dry-cleaning store for damage (loss) to his *pair of trousers*, thus not honoring the store's "satisfaction guarantee" slogan, and sued for $54,000,000 (that's fifty-four million dollars, 54 followed by six zeroes!). When I first heard about it, I thought it was all a joke. But it was not. The evening news flashed on the TV screen the image of this *expensive* attorney, in his *expensive* suits, making an *expensive* and fragrantly *GREEDY* claim for a mere pair of slacks. And I truly wondered where and how did he get his business law degree. (My daughter is also a business-law attorney.) Truly, such audacious exhibition of greed makes a mockery of the spirit of law as well as any sense of human decency toward fellow men. And I wondered, too, if he was a pro-fesssed Christian, or a member of another faith, whether Buddhist, Islamic, or whatever, and if he had ever heard of a Bible passage:

> *"What does it profit a man if he gain the whole world*
> *[but] lose his own soul?!"*

Would it ever be possible that one day the world would be free of greed?

Truly, the day the world is without man's greed would also be the day when the Kingdom of God is realized on this earth. For without greed, there would be no poor, without greed, there would be no war, and without greed, the sick, the afflicted, the widows and the fatherless would be cared for as well as all others. Surely, without greed, there would be no need for fighting over power and wealth. For, without greed, there would be true equality, and the *Peaceable* Kingdom shall finally be realized on this earth, and we don't have to wait until we are all dead to enter that peaceful kingdom.

I cannot imagine a world that is more peaceable, more beautiful, more God's-kingdom like, than a world that is without the greed of man.

17

The Lessons from the Land of My Ancestors

The China I visited in 1990 is not the China today. The U.S. government has classified it as one of the "emerging" countries, no longer a "third-world" country. Americans are good at labeling other people and other countries. By calling China "emerging" it meant that the people and the government no longer needed the *modern* Jesuit priests to point out their weakness in the knowledge and government polity.

Indeed China had gone through some of the most difficult times since the Ming dynasty. During the late Qing dynasty (nineteenth century), they had to endure the shame of the Opium War, followed by numerous unfair and humiliating treatises that were imposed on China by Western countries (including Germany, France, England and America), literally at gunpoint. Since the founding of the Republic of China, ending more than two millennia of imperial dynastic rule, China again had to withstand and survive the invasion of Japan. At the end of World War II, the Russians came into Manchuria and Korea to usurp all the establishment of imperial Japan there, and continued their claim of war booty into China, dismantling northern China's factories and railroads, or whatever they could transport, back to Russia. Then, the civil war between the Communists and the Nationalists tore China apart, and the Russians, intending to make China a Stalin satellite colony, joined hands with China's Communist leadership and imposed an intense political and educational oversee over China.

The national woes, alas, were not always from foreign invasion. During the decade-long "Great Proletarian Cultural Revolution" (1966-76) called by Chairman Mao Tzedong and his actress-singer wife, the whole of China suffered one of the greatest destructions known in all human history. Countless Red Guard troops, most of them mere teen-age students, blindly obeyed the Chairman's call to arms, to reform the nation and to rid the nation of its ills, called "four olds." The *four olds* were specifically identified and targeted by the four self-appointed guardians of China's new culture. After the Cultural Revolution, the members of this supreme committee of arts and culture were branded as the "Gang of Four" (which included the Chairman's wife), forced to stand trial, and purged. But before the tremendous damage of national scale was done, these youthful zealots roamed every city and every village, without any fear of reprisal, since they had the blessing of, and were carrying out the direct order of Supreme Chairman Mao Tzedong.

But for about ten fearful and miserable years between 1966 and 1976, millions of Chinese—nearly all intellectuals, or wealthy—were made to stand trial, being accused of being "anti-revolutionary," and were imprisoned or executed. Among them were China's leading thinkers, intelligentsia, educators and professors; some of them were the very parents and teachers of these young and accusing hoodlums who were suddenly given license to accuse, arrest, convict, and force anyone suspected of harboring Western thoughts to atone for their "crime against Chinese people" by surrendering all their earthly possessions, positions, properties, and even lives. A worse fate awaited the landlords; they were branded the enemy of the people and were summarily imprisoned and executed. In one estimate, over twelve million Chinese died during the Cultural Revolution.

In 1990 I set my foot on Chinese soil for the first time in my life. During the conference, sponsored by the newly established *Society for Research in American Music* (SRAM), I learned that about half of the faculty members of the famed Shanghai Conservatory—arguably the best music conservatory in the entire Far East—had either committed suicide or died in prison during the Cultural Revolution. The only crime they were charged with was that they propagated *Western* music and *Western* thinking. However, they did not regard Russia as one of the Western countries and, hence, things Russian—language, science, music, educational system, *etc*. were adopted. Apparently, the directional reference such as east or west was purely for convenience.

But Chinese are—always have been and always will be—a resilient people. After all, they have survived as one nation and one people for over five millennia. Soon after Chairman Mao died, and his wife and the other members of the Gang of Four were properly disposed, China quickly regained its vitality, under a more pragmatic national policy of Premier Deng Xiaoping, and began to emerge at a remarkable pace as a viable equal in the League of Nations. As expected, once again the Western nations saw a new opportunity, and began to explore ways to reach (to) this new China, to see how they, the individual entrepreneurs as well as government agencies, could profit from twentieth-century Cathay, as the diehard traders had once done several centuries ago by treading the full length of the Silk Roads.

Emerging from the ashes of war and the bloodshed of the Cultural Revolution and, more recently, smarting from the world criticism of the Chinese government's handling of the infamous *Tian-An-Men* Square incident, China was quick to come to the realization that there was an enormous amount of catching up to do, not only in technology and scientific and artistic learning but, more importantly, in better managing international political, commercial and economic affairs in wheeling and dealing with the West. In short, the Chinese government has come to realize that, while ideology is still important, one must be sufficiently pragmatic. In order to become decent and respectable player in the world's arena, even the old guards of the communist party have realized that "man shall not live by '*ism*' alone." It might be that this wise and foresighted Premier was at least in some ways influenced by his own son attending an American university on the East Coast.

Premier Deng Xiaoping, while barely five feet tall, certainly had his eyes set on high mountains and farther horizons. At the convention of the national delegation, he casually quipped, even as if in passing, that "To be rich is glorious!" The entire China knew that an important person such as Premier simply would not quip casually, that every word, every little phrase carries a profound implication. Hence, these words of Premier Deng instantly became the "lamp" to Chinese feet, and the whole China responded in one thunderous "Amen!" (No, they really didn't say "*Amen*;" it's just my loose interpretation of the national psyche). And, I suppose, the 1990 conference to which I was invited to participate was symptomatic of the new national posture, the nation's intensely focused desire and concerted effort to learn more about the West, and to become *bourgeois*-ishly rich. And the 2008 Olympics in Beijing will most assuredly let the whole world know that the new China has made an incredible climb and now has arrived at—or, at least, near—the summit of the world.

The conference I attended in 1990 was the first symposium of the newly founded *Society for Research in American Music*, held at Shandong Arts College in Jinan City. Two days after arriving in Beijing, Prof. Papastavrou (Syracuse University) and I took an eight-hour train ride to Jinan, and we were overwhelmed, even embarrassed, by the most generous accommodations. A chief chef was exclusively assigned to us, whose duty it was to prepare the three daily meals for just the two of us during the duration of the conference, and there were no more than two or three other people sitting with us at the table; one was the interpreter (more for Prof. Papastavrou's sake), and the other conference representatives, taking turns to get acquainted with their first "encounter with the West."

Among the most memorable experience for me, an Easterner who is now more Western in perspectives and tastes, were the two dinners. The first was the welcome dinner where conference officials and many delegates were also present, and the other was the farewell dinner, where all conference participants along with a number of distinguished guests were all gathered for the occasion. Of all the exquisitely prepared and genuinely Chinese dishes that were served, a couple stood out and will always stay in my memory. One was the turtle soup, and the other was a plate of deep fried grasshoppers. Grasshoppers tasted all right, crunchy and flavorful, nothing particularly unusual, except that the thought of eating those little critters was unusually "exciting." But, the turtle soup! Without a doubt, it was the tastiest soup I have ever had in my entire life. No Cajun gumbo or French onion soup would ever come close to this incredibly smooth and divinely flavorful taste. Each person was served the soup in a rather large bowl, and in each bowl was a whole turtle submerged in the light creamy liquid. And it was one of those unforgettable experiences, to be able to lift completely and cleanly with just a gentle lift with chopsticks the whole of the top shell of the turtle that had been *slowly* cooked to absolute tenderness.

I was told that turtle soup was known as a longevity potion, and I recalled a scene in the movie *The Last Emperor* where, early in the movie, the old "empress"-dowager was near death and the entire court retinue was at her bedside, there was a huge, *timpani*-size bronze bowl standing next to the dowager's bed-couch, with steam (and, I am sure, fragrance, too) rising from the pot. If your eyes are quick enough, you could see the head of a *huge* turtle in that humongous bronze bowl, half submerged but unmistakably identifiable.

The conference lasted five whole days, and the entire session was rather ceremonial, as compared to professional conferences in the United States. The seating was in a large U-shaped arrangement, with comfortable individual couches in the front row, and "standard" (wooden or metal) chairs in the subsequent rows behind. Since I was an invited guest from a foreign country and was designated as a "consultant," I was seated in the front row, and feeling somewhat self-conscious. Sitting to my right was George Papastavrou (so I could whisper into his ears the details of the proceeding), and to my left was Mr. Sun Xuehwu, a professor from Xi'an Conservatory. Soon after, the meeting was under way. I took notice of Prof. Sun, for he posed penetrating questions to the paper presenters more than once, and his delivery was eloquent and articulate, with a resonant baritone voice. As I looked his way whenever he spoke, I began to notice too that he was a person of impressive appearance; sitting up straight, almost half a head taller than I, and handsome, with jet-black hair combed straight back, his eyebrows long and dark, and his nose more like Greek or American Indian than the generally "flatter-and-wider" southern Asian type.

After the long (over two hours) first session, there was a recess and serving of refreshments; I stood up, talked to George for a couple of minutes, and turned myself to greet Prof. Sun. He was just getting up, and I saw him push down two crutches, slowly get up and straighten himself up to my eye level. Catching me gazing at him, he smiled and extended his hand to shake mine. I couldn't remember what I said then; perhaps more like muttering in awkward Chinese to self-introduce. The truth is, I was a little dumbfounded, completely unaware, unsuspecting, and too surprised to discover that, in striking contrast to the upper half of his physical body, his legs were maimed, awkwardly twisted, and he walked most grotesquely, shuffling his legs with the aid of crutches.

During the next few days, I thought of asking him about his physical handicap, but couldn't muster enough courage to bring myself to ask what could be an awkwardly embarrassing question. But, on the last day of the conference, when the last session was over and there was time for a series of quick photo sessions and mingling with the conference participants and to say goodbye, I could not hold my curiosity any longer. Somewhat sheepishly, I finally asked Prof. Sun what had happened to his legs.

"O, this!" he said with a smile, looking down at his legs, then up and into my eyes. "Many years ago, during the Cultural Revolution, a band of Red Guards came to my house one day and broke my knees. But, "*mei-you shi-moh*" ("there isn't much to it")," he said with a gentle and genuine smile, then continued to ask me about something else, totally oblivious to my earlier question about his condition and about my curiosity.

I was deeply moved, not so much by what he had said but, rather, by *how* he had said it. Here is a man who had suffered a tragedy, a malicious cruelty done to him for no cause or justification. It was during one of the most horrendous periods in the history of modern China, and the pain and suffering was not due to foreign invasion but was committed by bands of totally misguided youthful hoodlums, waving the red book of Mao Tzedong and declearing war against all who had anything to do with the "old" and the West. (I even bought a copy of Chairman Mao's *Red Book*, just wanted to find out what he had written that had brought so much tragedy to the people of China).

Yet, here standing in front of me, Prof. Sun retold it simply, matter-of-factly, as if it was something not worth calling attention to, that it was more like a wind blew and a twig fell on his head. Or, even if it was more than that to him personally, he was saying—without putting it in so many words—that whatever had happened, life would go on, with or without him, that, in the final analysis, life will continue on just the same, that a man's life's calling is far greater than one incident that had happened on one particular day.

I left Jinan to return to Beijing to catch my return flight. But the day before leaving Beijing, I took time to visit another unforgettable person I had also met at the conference. That person was Prof. Xiao Shu-Xien, a most gracious lady, with a genuinely sincere but somewhat shy smile, and she was very diminutive (perhaps a little over four and half feet). She introduced herself to me one day, near the end of the conference, and said that she was a retired professor of composition (she was already in her eighties), now living with her son and his family in an apartment in a suburb of Beijing, and she invited me—almost insisted—to visit her before returning to the United States.

I took the city bus alone, an adventure in itself since I was totally unfamiliar with the city or its mass transportation system. After about half an hour of bus ride, I arrived at a less congested neighborhood; I walked across a bridge, following her directions. It was shortly after noon, and I saw several street workers sitting on the roadside, surrounding a makeshift "table"—actually a piece of wooden board plopped on top of a concrete block—playing the game of (Western) cards. Nearby I also saw drinking bottles and aluminum containers that I gathered to be their lunch boxes. "A game of cards after lunch, how relaxing," I thought to myself as I approached them. "May I watch?" I asked, and several answered in one accord, "*Dan-ran, dan-ran!*" ("Of course, of couse"), repeating the word several times, as Chinese are accustomed to doing when giving short answers. I couldn't tell what card game they were playing; actually I was more attracted by their jovial demeanor and candid behavior, not a shred of pretense, and utterly genuine. And I was struck by the fact that these Chinese street workers, who earned perhaps one or two US dollars for a day's labor (that was in 1990), could still find time and leisure in their heart to enjoy the simplest of pleasures in life. I watched their faces, glittering eyes, genuine smiles, and listened to their laughter of contentment.

And I felt a bit envious.

Walking further down the now less-well-maintained paved road, I found rows of apartment buildings, each building bearing a huge number high on the wall to identify an apartment which otherwise was totally indistinguishable from the next. Finally I found Prof. Xiao's apartment and rang the doorbell. Almost instantly, a fine looking young man, perhaps in his mid-teens, opened the door. I identified myself and was led into the small guest room and saw Prof. Xiao standing, waiting for me. We talked for a good while, sipping hot tea. After a while, she led me into another small room in the back of the apartment, and I saw that there were more bookshelves full of paper and scores than space to move around. We chatted yet another while, and I asked about her self, for several people at the conference had told me that she was a very famous person. With her gentle smile never fading from her face, Prof. Xiao told me in a slow, reflective pace that she studied composition at Beijing Central Conservatory, then went to Germany for graduate studies and, there, she met her future husband, an eminent German conductor, Hermann Scherchen.

Scherchen was a strong advocate for and the leading champion of 'new music,' and was involved in the preparation and the premiere of Schoenberg's *Pierrot Lunaire*. He lectured at the Musikhochschule (conservatory) and became conductor of the Leipzig Orchestra as well as the director of Frankfurt Museum Orchestra, and toured through-out Europe. When the Nazis came to power, new music was denounced as poisonous (Hitler did not like any music after Wagner), and Scherchen and his Chinese wife left Germany in 1933 and settled in Switzerland. After the war, Scherchen got the support of UNESCO (of the United Nations) to open one of the earliest electronic music studios in the world. Because of his increasing professional standing and artistic status, he was invited to guest conduct in the United States, the New York Philharmonic (when Toscanini had taken ill), and also the Philadelphia Orchestra. Then he was offered the conductor's posi-tion. However, the New York Phil made it clear to him that his Chi-nese wife was NOT to accompany him to the United States. It was already in the mid-1950s, about ten years after the war ended. No mat-ter. To the Board of Directors of the New York Philharmonic, a Chi-nese was still a Chinese, never an equal in the eyes of the Westerners or Jews. Thereupon Scherchen declined the offer and chose to remain in Switzerland with his wife. (Today, the daughter of Hermann and Shusien, Tona Scherchen-Hsiao, is a composer still living in Switzer-land.)

About ten years later, Scherchen died, and Prof. Xiao returned to her homeland in the hope that she could now make a contribution to rejuvenate arts and music in postwar China. That was 1966, the year that the Cultural Revolution began, and she was summarily rounded up with others and sent to the labor camp in the collective farm, where she spent nearly ten years in forced hard labor as a farmhand. She told me her life's story, while her smile never faded from her delicately gen-tle and graceful face. She showed me their photos, his scores, and his letters.

I walked out of her apartment and into the bright streets outside. But the gentle late afternoon breeze did nothing to clear my head that was full of thoughts, about music, about life, about Germans and Chinese and Americans, about Nazis, the New York Philharmonic, the Cultural Revolution, and about the East and West. It was OH so difficult to comprehend the minds of men, to understand the reasons for their actions, of the Red Guards, of the Nazis. But of the Board of Directors of the New York Phil, the organization that is devoted to promoting noble music for the common people?! I thought I heard angels weeping. Or was it my own sobbing?

On my flight home, along (no longer in the company of George Papastavrou), I reflected on Prof. Sun, and the lovely, diminutive and utterly gracious Prof. Xiao. I went over and over again the stories of their encounters and especially on what and how they had related the tragedies that befell them. But, most of all, I reflected on what they had shown me, and how they had allowed me an opportunity to glimpse the incomparable and indomitable integrity of their spirit.

And I thought of myself, and felt utterly ashamed. In flight, some thirty thousand feet up in the sky, I was so overcome with shame that I literally sobbed (quietly, so not to arouse the notice of my next-seat passengers). I had read many biographies of historical greats. But, for the first time, I saw my smallness, my pettiness about daily things; about how easily I would become upset by things so trivial, when a fax didn't go through immediately, when a Xerox machine produced poor quality copy, when toast got a bit too dark, when traffic was a bit too slow, too long, when a student's response was not what it should be, or when a committee member seemed not to know when to shut up during the meeting, those annoyances which, in the final analysis, are all so petty, so insignificant and so inconsequential. I saw myself as so prone to get preoccupied with myself, to let small things fill my mind, that I lost sight of the more important things in life, for me as well as for others.

I thought, too, how often we waste precious moments of our life in self-pity, and how sad when we let that self-pity consume us, diverting our energy from the truly worthwhile task of life. I thought of a dear colleague of mine, Dr. Samuel Scott, a brilliant man, upright, insightful, eloquent and straight talking, though a bit arrogant at times. He was amicable and sincere to his friends, but he could also be unforgiving. As soon as he detected a bit of insincerity or deceitfulness in another person, he would not even bother to extend a mere cordial "hello." For a number of years, his annual review by the committee of his peers was far from "meritorious" and, as a result, his salary began to lag behind that of his colleagues, and his rank stayed the same. Every spring, from about late March to April, it was painful for me to see him agonize over the absence of recognition of his work by his own peers sitting in judgment on the committee, and he would audibly lament how he was again going to bring the disappointing news to Carmen, his wife. And I watched him becoming increasingly bitter with each passing year. Still, while he had always regarded me as his best friend (and I his), no amount of my persuasion seemed to make him see the need to change his old ways. He retired early—I suppose that it was his way of showing defiance—and two years later he passed away, his mind still active and brilliant, but his heart bitter and broken. I mourned for his inability—or unwillingness—to see that life is nothing less than a gift, that we fail but ourselves and the ones we love if we cannot let go of things or feelings that make us unhappy.

How was China able to endure all the shame, adversities and defeats throughout the centuries, and reemerge tenacious, unscathed, if not always victorious? I believe it was because of the resilience of the collective personality of the people, to learn from history and to learn from others, even the adversaries. And I remembered the lessons explained to me while walking the hallways where Confucius once discoursed his disciples (in *peripatetic* fashion, as did Plato and Aristotle), and while visiting his memorial gravesite during the tour right after the SRAM conference: that the wisdom (of his teaching) was an emphasis in moderation, patience, accommodation and, above all, *ren*—literally *benevolence* but also, on a deeper level, the "humility of spirit." Of the latter, I was reminded a saying of Confucius, the greatest teacher mankind has ever known, that

"Whenever I walk with another man, he is my teacher,
for there always will be something I can learn from him."

18

The Joy and Mystery of My Rising Sun [Son]

Never was there a moment in my life that brought me as much joy as the morning of June 9, 1987. Shortly after 10 o'clock, my son Geoffrey was born. I was at my wife's bedside in the delivery room and holding her hand when he emerged, and it was a bit unusual, I thought, that he did not let out the usual loud cry of a baby coming out into the world. But he weighed in at about seven pounds, perfectly healthy, and that was all that mattered. Round and red faced (Japanese call a baby *aka-chian*, meaning "the little *red* one") and eyes shut, he was peaceful and content in his mother's tight embrace. Her countenance was radiant and all smiles, without the slightest sign of weariness that she had just given birth to a child. For our son had brought us a joy of unspeakable measure. Soon, the nurses told me that I should leave the room, now that I had seen that both the baby and the mother were in excellent condition, and they needed rest. I walked out of the hospital room lingeringly, fearing that if I walked too fast, the scenes of my son's birth would fade away.

I got in the car, but I didn't want to just go home alone. I was too excited, and wanted to shout out to the whole world and let them know that "I have a son!" Instead, I went to the mall, and bought myself a nice pipe and bought the best tobacco cuts the store had. Walking around the mall and puffing the pipe, I kept on repeating to myself the same phrase, as if to make myself believe that it truly had happened, that now "I have a son!"

I was already in my fifties when Geoffrey was born, and I regarded my son as no less than a gift from above. Holding him each night while trying to woo him to sleep, I would gaze into his chubby face, and saw myself, or, rather, I saw the *extension of my life.* There was an undeniable tie between the son and the father. And as he grew, I saw that this tie was not just something in my imagination. He was and is the continuation of my life; he was—and is—like me in so many ways. Even my students who saw Geoffrey for the first time had said, in many different ways, "he is every bit like you, Dr. Cho. Just look at him; you can tell he is *your* son."

I suppose this is an "Oriental" thing, to attach so much joy and importance to the birth of a son. For example, there is a saying in China that "the greatest *indebtedness* for a man to his ancestors is not to have a son." The connotation is clear enough; not having a son is tantamount to letting the lineage of the family name cease forever. For this reason, the greatest responsibility for a wife was to give a son to her husband. I know of several families where the wives felt obligated—or were forced—to continue bearing children until finally she gave birth to a son. Then and only then would the wife be regarded as having fulfilled her highest obligation to her husband's ancestral (*i.e.,* the family) name.

When I was in Hong Kong for a two-year visiting professor appointment, a colleague of mine who was awarded a Fulbright Fellowship to spend a semester in Shengyang Conservatory (northeast China) had told me that, nearly every morning, one could find a newborn baby girl or two carefully wrapped but otherwise abandoned at the doorsteps of a central hospital, at times with notes pinned on the baby's clothes but more often than not without any clue. In the country where "one-family-one-child" is a government policy in attempt to resolve China's perennial problem of overpopulation, parents whose first child is a girl would face the grave dilemma of choosing between obeying the childbirth law of the government and fulfilling the dictate of tradition regarding family obligation. Many, especially those in the rural and more tradition-bound regions, would have no hesitation in following the way of honoring ancestors. Orphanages all across China are full of healthy but unwanted baby girls, with a much smaller number of male children who, without exception, are severely handicapped.

On one of our sightseeing tours across China, we befriended a young American couple (the husband was a medical doctor) on the train; they became curious because a Chinese boy—our son Geoffrey—was speaking fluent English. We began to chat and quickly learned that they were on their way to adopt a baby girl. Literally thousands of "orphaned"—or, more accurately, abandoned—baby girls are adopted by kind-hearted American couples, who would give new hope and a completely changed perspective of life to those little babies who were given up by their own parents only because they were born of the "wrong" sex.

I had a daughter before Geoffrey was born, and I poured my love and care on her. But, when turning forty and then fifty, I had quietly resigned myself while content, without any feeling of not fulfilling my traditional obligation, that there would be no son in my life. After all, my younger brother had two sons, and the lineage of the Cho family name will securely remain. Then, Geoffrey came into my life. And as it was all so totally unexpected, the joy was truly indescribable. Besides, he was—and still is—so much like me!

When Geoffrey was in kindergarten, his teacher told us on the day of the Christmas program that Geoffrey sang the loudest in the class, adding that his classmates would often chide him not to sing so loud. I had to apologize to the teacher, and offered an explanation that Geoffrey sang loud because he always saw me leading the congregational singing in the church, where I always sang in front of a microphone in order that the whole church could follow my lead. The teacher then said, "No wonder. Actually, Geoffrey sings very well, better than the other children. He learns songs so well and so quickly, and he always sings in tune." I didn't have the courage to tell the teacher that Geoffrey should be very musical, *naturally*, like his father.

When I accepted a visiting professor position in Hong Kong, my wife and I were unsure if Geoffrey should come along right away, or should wait at home with his mother until she finished her graduate degree, and then join me in Hong Kong later. We decided to ask Geoffrey his opinion, having just finished the first grade. Without hesitation, he said "I want to go with Daddy." My heart leaped for joy over my son's decision, but I kept the feeling to myself, lest my wife would feel slighted. Besides, I wanted him to come along because I wanted him to get acquainted with things of his cultural heritage. Earlier that year, Geoffrey came home from school one day and asked, "Daddy, the teacher said I am a *mi-nor-i-ty*. Why am I a mi-nor-i-ty?" And I thought to myself: over a quarter of mankind is Chinese, and we are regarded as a minority people?

It was from that moment that I knew I must give my son an opportunity to live among his own ethnic kind, in a traditional cultural environment, where he could learn and experience what it was to be a Chinese, so that he would be proud of his own ethnic and cultural heritage. Granted, Hong Kong was a British colony (three more years to go before being returned to China), and people there speak Cantonese, a very different kind of dialect from Mandarin (the *putong-hoa*, the official Chinese language). But Chinese are Chinese, the same everywhere, and I wanted my son to be able to come out of a life's experience and to regard himself as *Chinese*-American (*i.e.*, Chinese first), rather than American-Chinese.

For awhile, I had feared that Geoffrey would have to be sent home, because we were told by the school officials that all the international schools were full to capacity, that there simply wasn't any room for him. After a week of desperate search, I was introduced to an officer in the Department of Education, in the *Central* district of Hong Kong (island, as opposed to the *New Territory* that was a part of Mainland China). With only a telephone call from his office, Geoffrey was admitted to *Shatin Junior College*, an international school which has both the academy and the primary school. I had forgotten that there was that Oriental magic in expediting things of even the most difficult nature: it is called *goanxi*—"connection."

Thank God for *goanxi* that wrought wonders. For Shatin Junior College was right across the highway from Hong Kong Baptist University Senior Staff Quarters where Geoffrey and I had taken residence and, from our sixth-floor apartment veranda, we could see the schoolyard and even his third grade classroom (Geoffrey was placed a grade ahead). Wearing the red-stripe shirt school uniform, Geoffrey became a Hong Kong student, in a school where, even as an international school, about 90 percent of the students were Chinese. Every morning, I would walk him to school, *very carefully* crossing the highway (there were no traffic lights on the curved and sloped highway, and Hong Kong drivers were, well, rather Chinese, who knew well that their cars were equipped with horns but seemed not to remember that the cars have brakes, too). I would then hurry back to the apartment and wave to him from the veranda. And he would always remember to look my way, and raise his little hand to acknowledge.

For six months, I was both the father and mother to Geoffrey. I kept the apartment, prepared breakfast, cooked the evening meal, ironed his school uniform, helped him with his homework, held him close on the couch while watching TV, gave him a bath, and put him to bed. During the weekends, we would go out to explore Hong Kong, from the ultra-modern shopping malls (Newtown Plaza was then called the largest interconnected shopping center in the world, and was Geoffrey's favorite "hunting ground"), to the very traditional Chinese markets in the narrow and often wet back streets, where chicken and pig heads were hung on stalls, and shopkeepers would chop up live fish right in front of your eyes, filling every detail of your order. Seeing this sight for the first time, Geoffrey was almost in tears and turned away. But he recovered quickly and, steadying himself, he went back and looked at the very scene he had walked away from just a few seconds ago.

We also explored or otherwise *exploited* the international cuisines that Hong Kong offered and oh, how Chinese loved to eat. You could literally go out any time of the day or night, and find food stalls offering anything and everything from hamburgers (catered mostly to the younger generations) to ginger-flavored chicken-liver soup (my favorite is the coagulated chicken-blood soup but, please, don't tell my Jewish friends), and from pizzas to raw-fish *sashimi* delicacies, at an amazingly affordable price. The price of pizza was rather exorbitant, for a size much smaller and the flavor most ordinary. And we felt it rather un-Chinese to waste money on a poor imitation of China's *dabin* (the "big and flat cake") that Marco Polo had introduced to Europe from China several centuries before. Within the first month, Geoffrey had acquired a taste for *sushi* and, especially, the *sashimi* and *escargots* (that's snails), and he was only seven years and four months old. That made his father very proud.

After Geoffrey's mother came to join us in Hong Kong, we took advantage of geographic proximity to travel across China, north to Beijing and Xi'An (which is China's oldest capital, famous for the

Emperor Qin's royal tomb with several thousand life-size terra cotta soldiers), and south to Shanghai, Hangzhou, Suchuan to Macao. For we both wanted to expose our son to all the historical legends and cultural treasures from China's five thousand year history. We climbed the Great Walls, and sailed down the famous Li River.

Some of the most memorable moments from the travel came from totally unexpected encounters. Once, stepping off the modern, air-conditioned tour bus, we found ourselves surrounded by a band of children in rags, all hands stretched toward the tourists. Geoffrey took out some money from his pockets and gave it to the begging children, then saw a boy who was terribly deformed, also asking Geoffrey for a handout. Geoffrey didn't have any more money, and I stepped in to help. A few moments later, while we were walking toward the plush restaurant for another sumptuous meal, Geoffrey said something that I would always remember. Looking up at me and with tears in his eyes, he said quietly, "Daddy, life is not fair, is it?"

After another year and a half in Hong Kong, we returned to Texas, back once again to the father-and-son team (his mother had to stay behind in Hong Kong for another year and a half to complete the terms of her contractual obligation). After awhile, I began to notice that Geoffrey was not doing quite as well in school; his grades were fine, but he was not a happy child. He had never confided to me—and only later did we find out—that, because he had skipped one grade, he didn't have any of his friends from the first grade in the same class, and he also was the youngest. The bigger and older boys in the class were bent on showing this lad newly returned to Texas that he was an outsider, a loner, an easy pick to push around. And the teachers seemed oblivious. Once outgoing, happy and talkative, Geoffrey became quiet and reserved almost overnight. But, through it all, he showed us another side of him that we never knew he had in him: resilience and tenacity, an inner strength to bear, cope with and to resolve problems on his own and in his own terms.

Two more years in elementary school after returning to Texas, he entered the newly built middle school across the highway from our house, and he was once again a happy camper. He excelled in school, and learned quickly to play violin, and won himself a first prize in solo competition. After two years at the middle school, and two more years at high school (ninth and tenth grades), he was accepted into a special program that allowed students to combine the last two years of high school with the first two years of college. Through this program (TAMS, for Texas Academy of Mathematics and Science), he will be entering university as a junior while still seventeen, and graduating from the university before his twentieth birthday. That would make his *old* dad very happy.

But, far more than any of the achievements in academic subjects and extracurricular activities, the greater source of my joy is in recognizing Geoffrey's attitude toward himself, toward those around him, and toward life. I see that he is a deep thinker, much more mature than many young people I have known (and I have known literally thousands in my more than three and a half decades of university teaching), and is neveer boastful of his accomplishments.

One day in Geoffrey's high school year, his mother saw by a sheer chance a certificate in his desk drawer. Taking a quick glance, she shouted, "Geoffrey, what is *this*?" "Oh, it's *nothing*, Mom," he said nonchalantly. "*Nothing*? You should be very proud of things like this, and should have shown it to us!" It was a certificate recognizing him as the first in academic standing in the high school sophomore class of six hundred seventy-some students.

In our quiet conversations, I could feel that he has set his aim in achieving the highest goal he is capable of, in the arenas where he chooses to compete with confidence, and he sets his aim not in the present, or immediate future, but at some point far ahead. But, more than all these, my greatest joy and comfort is to see that he, too, feels the unmistakably close bond between himself and his father, and believes that to "honor and respect the father" is a true virtue of a son, not because of what the father is or what he has done, but simply because he is *his* father.

There are many things I want to share with Geoffrey, to teach him a lesson or two from my life's experience: above all else, he must believe in himself; he must cast his vision far and high, and not be overly concerned with things immediately surrounding or in front of him; he must never desire immediate gratification, that life is a long and arduous journey, where the degree of success and happiness is measured not so much by things immediately visible, but by how he regards himself; to achieve one's life's goals requires persistence and tenacity, not to be discouraged by temporary setbacks or a few disappointments along the way; in the final analysis, one can truly be content so long as he believes that he has done his best; that to have a true measure of self-respect is to also give others their due respect, and to be kind to and considerate of others; he must always be able to look at himself in the mirror and see in there an honest, sincere, and upright man.

But, somehow, I feel that he already has in him these same perspectives of life. I feel that, in spite of his age, he has already learned some of the fundamental lessons of life, that there is really no need for his old dad to worry about how well he will live his life.

Among my personal treasured items is a father's-day card from Geoffrey when he was still in junior high, and a typed note inside the card. The note reads as follows (un-edited unless otherwise noted):

Even though this card does say many things that I agree with,
it does not even begin to convey the thanks and gratitude that

I owe to you, and even after looking through many cards all over the store, I know that none of those cards will be able to. You have always been there for me, Dad, and I know that you always will—and I promise on my part that I will always give my very best in return, no matter what it takes.

I know that there have been many times where I disappointed you, and also many times where I made you angry—but only in these past few months have I finally realized that every glare, every voice raised, every push, was not done in outrage, but rather in the care and love that you hold for me, [when] seeing that I'm not at my best. I will try my hardest to never let that happen again, to never disappoint you, but this regrettably is something that I cannot fully promise.

However, the promise I give you today, Dad, is also my life's goal to achieve.

I promise you that I will do anything and everything it takes to make you proud of me.

When I'm praying, there are many times where I thank God so much for blessing me with such a father, for I myself still can't undersand what I ever did to deserve someone like you. I think of myself and all the failures that I have done, and it still hurts so much to think of how much of a disappointment I am. You deserve the perfect son, the smartest son, the best looking son, and I am sorry that I am not these things, nor ever will be.

But that's one of the things that I love you so much for. It takes a very special person to accept me, it takes a very special person to love me, and I'm so thankful that you do.

(the following sentence omitted)

You have made sure that I had everything I needed. You gave me so much more than I deserve, and I now realize that everything that you did, you did just for me, without any thought of expecting something in return.

Your integrity, veracity, trustworthiness, altruism: all the qualities
that make you that father I know, is something that I myself hope
one day to achieve.
You have set an example that I'll follow for life. You've shown me
to do what is right; to give my best, to show respect; and your
words will always ring true in my head and heart.
Thank you for always being there for me, and I promise that one day
I'll make you proud enough so that you'll be able to say with pride
"That's my son."
Happy Father's Day! I love you, Dad.
Geoffrey (signed)

Since then, I have told Geoffrey several times that he was not entirely correct in his understanding of his father's mind. For his father knows that he already has the best son a man could ever hope to have, that his father has been—and will always be—proud of his son, not because of his achievements, but because his father already knows that he believes in himself, and that he has complete trust in the love of his parents. Truly, what more could parents expect from their children?

That a child of mine has formulated such personal beliefs, nearly all on his own, that he already possesses a measure of wisdom, is a mystery to me. And that I have such a son is the source of my unfading joy and profound comfort. He is the precious gift to me from above. He is a bright light in my life. Indeed, he is my son (sun).

19

Life, Liberty, and the Pursuit of Happiness

There is a large rubbing of Confucius' image over the desk in my office. And, for many years, I also had a copy of the *Magna Carta* (the "Great Charter") posted next to Confucius. It is my way of expressing "The Best of the East Meets the Best of the West." Created in the early thirteenth century, the *Magna Carta* was one of the earliest pronouncements of human rights that King John was forced by the democracy-minded barons to sign. With this *Great Charter* in place, the ordinary citizens of England were guaranteed their fundamental rights and privileges, even before the common people were regarded important enough to need a surname. Since then, history has witnessed that other nations have followed suit, as in France and the United States. In China, there was never such an official pronouncement. Instead, this same exhortation of basic human rights was articulated in an article called "*Li Yun Da Tong Pian*" by Confucius. In whatever languages these statements were written, these were and still remain the most preciously eloquent testimony of the best of human wisdom. For they are the *manifesto* of the great thoughts and noble spirits of man; they are the pleas, the prayers, and hopes of *all* mankind. Without these pronouncements and guarantees, mankind is no better than the beasts in the wild.

About fifteen years after coming to the United States, I applied for U.S. citizenship and, to prepare for the exam and interview, I studied, at least cursorily, U.S. history and the Constitution. The noble, powerful and eloquent statements in the *Preamble* moved me, and I was deeply grateful that I would now be among the citizenry of the land where the law of the government gives guarantees to a man's "*life, liberty, and pursuit of happiness.*" Just like the Ten Commandments given to the Israelites, these are the laws that are given to the people in the United States, and no man, not even a government agency or anyone in a position of power, can refute. So long as there is the United States on the surface of this earth, these constitutional rights of the citizenry will forever be guaranteed. But, of course, unlike the Ten Commandments where there are so many "*thou shalt nots,*" the U.S. Constitution is primarily the "thou shalt" sort; thou shalt be *free*, and thou shalt be free to pursue *happiness*.

There have been times, however, when I was not altogether sure about the American forefathers' wisdom in including the phrase "the pursuit of happiness" in the Constitution. What does it really mean? Would or could the government ever guarantee the happiness of its citizenry, or their ways in pursuing and realizing happiness? Could the government define and set any standards or boundary of happiness? What would make a person happy, and when would a person be *finally* happy? Or does it mean that each person is *free to pursue* happiness in whatever means and ways he sees fit?

The very first time I came to a small measure of appreciation of the *American* idea of "pursuit of happiness" was in a casual remark by a TEAM missionary to Taiwan, Mr. Leland Haggerty (from Seattle, WA), an electrical engineer who also was a fine singer, published composer and experienced conductor; in short, a most valuable Jack-of-all-trades kind of person in the mission field. One evening during our choir rehearsal, he turned to his daughter who was leaving for a party and said "*Have fun!*" Have fun, have a good time, enjoy, and be happy. And how Americans love to have fun and, it seems, everything is done in the spirit of "having fun." Americans are world famous as practical jokers, experts in having fun and at the expense of others. Have a good time and thus "be happy," especially if that happiness can be had without paying dues, can receive rewards without first putting in effort worthy of the rewards.

Many years ago, my mother-in-law came to stay with us for about two months. It was her first trip to the Land of Opportunity, and everything was strangely different and exciting. During the hours while we were at work and children were at school, my in-law enjoyed watching all the daytime soap operas and game shows. There were *The Price is Right* and *The Wheel of Fortune*, and she was fascinated by the wild behavior and unbridled jubilation of the people caught up in the frenzy of the shows. But, most of all, she could not believe that these games actually gave out the astonishing sum of prize money, ranging from a few thousand to tens of thousands of dollars. "All that money given away! It must be just make-believe."

Yes, make belief. And, in the United States, the pursuit of happiness is often in the form of dreaming and chasing after make-believe happiness. We have the state-run lottery, and every youngster—or oldster—who could sing and dance *a little* give themselves to believing that they have a shot at winning big on the likes of *Americas Got Talent* and *American Idol.* Even if you cannot sing or dance, but you think that your IQ is high enough, you could dream of winning big on the TV show *Who Wants To Be A Millionaire?* The whole nation is ablaze with the pursuit of happiness, and the whole country is in the gambling mentality. The pursuit of happiness by hook or by crook; and,

America seems to produce more crooks than all other industrial nations combined.

Nearly every day we hear on the evening news about stories of the most ingenious schemes or scams, often with the elderly and the poor as hapless victims. As the victims are often of lower social strata, no government agencies or lawyers who had sworn to uphold justice and to heal the ills of society would be particularly concerned with or interested in seeking justice on behalf of these victims of the zealous "pursuers of happiness." Meanwhile, we all continue to wish on our *stars* for our share of luck and happiness.

Even if we could not compete or win on game shows, we could at least dream, hope, and pray. We are easily convinced that, as in *Ned Washington*'s lyrics (in the 1940 movie *Pinocchio*),

> When you wish upon a star,
>
>> makes no difference who you are.
>
> Anything your heart desires will come to you
>
> If your heart is in a dream,
>
>> no request is too extreme.

not quite willing to accept the fact that children's fairly tales do not—if ever—translate into real life occurrences. You want to wish upon a star as dreamers do, casting our wish upon a star, and praying as if God manages the gambling table, or wishing that you *are* that stars, those rich and wealthy, young, beautiful and famous—whatever qualifies the star to be a star. In so wishing, we seldom consider personal virtue of stars (if they possess any), but only dream that you would be like the one who has things that make them famously a star, or the lucky few who have won the lottery, or a million dollars on a TV game show. After a while, we began to be *possessed* by the thought of becoming rich and famous, and wondered "why can't *I* be that person?" Consumed by jealousy and envy, some would feel that they have been short-changed, that this world is unfair, that they too should be entitled to a share of that happiness. Unable to realize their dreams, they would resort to pursuit of happiness at all cost, by shortcut measures: cheat, steal, or rob. Many others would simply give up, cease to see any sense in making any effort toward a more realistic pursuit of happiness, toward achieving a sense of accomplishment, even through sweat and hard work. In either case, the result is often a disillusionment, despondency, and dissatisfaction, toward self and toward those around him, including his immediate family. And the fruit from life's disappointment is often sad and even tragic.

Perhaps this was not the intention of our founding fathers, or that the emphasis was on freedom of life, and freedom in putting in the effort to pursue life's rewards, rather than "happiness." But it is a fact that the United States has become a nation of gamblers on all levels, in money, in power, in everything that we think would make us happy. And in the pursuit of happiness, we as a people and as a nation have lost a moral and ethical statue. Although still the wealthiest and most powerful, we the Americans are seen as arrogant, aggressive, opportunistic, but short in virtue and wisdom. It is sad that, today, few people in the world would regard America as trustworthy as leader of nations, and our international credence is below the People's Republic of China.

But, what is Happiness? How can we define Happiness? Perhaps there are as many answer to this question as the number of people in this country of gamblers. And I am afraid that "satisfaction" could never be *satisfactorily* defined because there is *no limit to satisfaction*. For as the *Good Book* says (am I beginning to sound like Tevye the dairyman in *Fiddler On the Roof?*),

"All the toil of man is for his mouth,
yet his appetite is never satisfied." (Ecc. 6:7).

There was a poor farmer in China long ago who had toiled for years yet was not able to better his life, not having enough to eat half of the year, and not able to keep warm in the winter. One day he sat down on a tree stump at the corner of his little plot of land, wiped the sweat off his head, as he often did, to get a moment of rest from toil. On this particular day, he lifted his eyes and poured his heart to god with all his complaints: "I have toiled for years but barely am able to survive. Why have I not been entitled to even a little blessing that so many others take for granted?" The next day, while he was plowing, a rabbit dashed out of the bushes and ran straight onto the tree stump, and dropped dead right in front of him. The farmer picked up the rabbit, and could hardly believe what he saw. The rabbit was a big, fat, fully mature male. Excited, the farmer left his plow behind and dashed to the market, and sold the rabbit to a butcher for an amount of money which was more than his half year's earning from back-breaking hard toil. He lifted his eyes and heart and thanked the heaven. He knew at that moment that this was a sign that heaven had heard his prayers, and heaven is telling him that hard toil was for stupid farmers and simpletons. He knew that henceforth he was going to be smarter, that all he needed to better his life's lot was to cast his luck on his stars (or stump), to sit at the corner of his land and wait for the next rabbit to come dashing out and hit against the tree. So he sat there, and days and months passed, and no rabbit came. When he woke up from his wishing and dreaming, he discovered that his little farmland had turned to hard clay, and nothing grew. And he died of starvation.

There is another folk tale from China: A rich old man knew that his earthly days were numbered, and was worried that his three sons who had never learned the frugality of life would not be able to manage his wealth wisely after his death. One day he called his sons to his side, and posed to each of his sons the question: "How would you arrange the funeral of your father?"

The eldest son extolled his father's life's years of hard labor and frugal virtue, and said that he would want an elaborate funeral, inviting all the town's people, to honor and memorialize the achievements of his father. Sadness came over his heart, and the father turned to the second son and asked the same question.

The second son essentially repeated the same as the first son, praising his father's life of rags to riches but he wanted the funeral to be private, to invite only kin folks and close friends for an occasion of a "family memorial." Still feeling sad in his heart, the father turned to the third son.

"Father," the youngest began, "I know you have worked so hard all your life, saved every penny where it was not absolutely necessary. Your wealth was paid for with your aches in your body and sweat on your forehead. For this reason, we as your heirs should put preservation of your wealth the utmost priority." The father's heart began to hum with joy.

"Although the funeral is important, it is primarily for eulogizing, and not an extravagant occasion. I would keep the funeral simple, inviting only the members of the immediate family and kin. No elaborate feasts and processions."

The youngest paused a while, then continued, slowly, as if in deep thought. "As for the coffin, I would even look for an inexpensive one, a plain square wooden-board container." The father was elated that his youngest son spoke such joy to his heart, and chimed in:

"Go on, my son. Tell me more of your funeral plans!"

"Well, father," the son again paused a little. "My brothers and I could carry the coffin, but I am hesitant to pay money to hire another person ..."

At that moment, the glad-hearted father was beside himself. Leaping out of his chair, he shouted,

"Don't worry, my son. Let ME help you carry!"

Rich or poor, learned or illiterate, CEO or cotton farmer, it seems that man is born to worry about his life's lot. While the rich worry about whether their millions will continue to multiply or at least be safe in the volatile market, or how to manipulate their stocks to get the better of others, many company employees worry about whether they would be the next victim in corporate downsizing, and the poor worry about where their next meal is going to come from. In essence, we all worry in search of the sure way in the pursuit of happiness.

There is a very interesting etymological perspective in the word *worry*. It is the history of how the word "worry" has become the psychology of worrying. The word originated in the Old English *wyrgan*, meaning 'to kill by strangulation.' It was a word used by hunters to describe how dogs would catch and overpower their prey; to "choke with a mouthful [bite], to seize by biting or shaking." Later, the word began to signify the "vicious but successful pursuit, or *an intense devouring of an object or a desire*." Eventually (in the 19th century) the word began to assume the meaning of "something that people do to themselves," a "*self-consuming passion*" not of the common animal sort, but of the *all-too-human behavior*. It is, as in the words of the renowned child psychotherapist Dr. Adam Phillips in his book *On Kissing, Tickling and Being Bored* (1993), the "*desirous ... often with a relentless weariness, by the minds of the troubled.*" In short, worry is a state of mental *possessed*ness. (The mind of Mr. Scrooge in Charles Dickens's *Christmas Carol* is a fine example of this mental possessed worrying.) How sad it is to realize that man is so prone to worrying, so easily driven to a frenzied state of mind in the pursuit of happiness.

I, too, had thought of the pursuit of happiness. Thinking about the pursuit of happiness was particularly intense during my life's darkest hours back in Chicago, when I was working as a janitorial-custodial, jack-of-all-trade repairman for an elderly Japanese couple. For a while I did not have enough money to continue my education. Alone in this foreign land, with no help in sight, and a future that seemed so uncertain and distant, I had often wondered how, when, or whether I would ever be happy. During the evening hours, quiet in my own room and in a rather meditative mood, I reflected on the reality of life, and asked myself *whether I would or could be happy if I were to be a handyman the rest of my living days*. I recalled and thought over what my father used to tell us children about *his* father's perspective of life: "I will sleep peacefully every night, after a day's hard toil, knowing that I have not been indebted to or shortchanged anyone."

In those days, I often recalled and reflected on the life lessons of great men. One of the stories I remembered was that of John D. Rockefeller (Sr.), the story I had read back in my high school days. Born to a household of six siblings of a hard working mother and an often-delinquent (and philandering) father, life was anything but comfortable. He did not finish high school, and took his first job as an apprentice bookkeeper, earning five cents a day. But his diligence and honesty soon led to a position of greater responsibility. For even as a young and lowly apprentice, he had believed in the importance of doing and *trying to be the best* whatever the task, no matter how menial the job.

I also recalled and reflected on a particular anecdote in Abraham Lincoln's presidency: The story has it that, late one night, his war minister rushed to the White House with urgent news. Hurrying down the hallway to the president's residence quarters, the minister was aghast and dismayed to find the president crouched down on the floor in a corner, polishing his own shoes. "Mr. President! I always wanted to tell you that some of your manners are most unbecoming. Why can't you have your staff polish your shoes?" Lincoln stood up and faced the minister smiling, and said calmly, "There are no low-class work; only low-class people." With that, he read the message of national importance, held in his shoe-polish-stained hand.

It was during this period that I also began to pray with words from verses in the Book of Proverbs:

> "Remove far from me falsehood and lying;
> *Give me neither poverty nor riches;*
> *Feed me with the food that is needful for me,*
> *Lest I be full, and deny thee, and say,*
> '*Who is the Lord?*'
> *Or lest I be poor and steal,*
> *And profane the name of my God.*"

And I was glad that I was able to answer my own question "whether I would or could be happy if I was to be a handyman the rest of my living days" with a genuinely affirmative YES. I may not live in a palatial residence, but I will be able to enjoy all the wonders of this world, and the interesting as well as challenging encounters of life, *with a peace of mind and a sense of self-respect and a dignity of independence.* And I began to conclude that, so long as I work hard and *complete each task to the best of my ability,* I shall never be in want. Beyond that, it is all a matter of perspective. For happiness is a state of mind, a state of being, and not a state of conditions.

And I began to see that, since there is no limit to man's desire, and material things are not what bring peace and joy to man's heart and soul, true happiness can be obtained in *being content*. Later, I found a verse in the Book of Ecclesiastes that seems to confirm that this perspective is right and just:

> *"Every man also to whom God has given wealth*
> *and possessions and power to enjoy them, and*
> *to accept his lot and find enjoyment in his toil—*
> *This is the gift of God."*

I think this same verse is rendered much clearer and more directly in the *Dictionary of Quotations* (Oxford University Press):

> *"To enjoy your work and to accept your lot in life—*
> *that is indeed a gift from God.*
> *The person who does that will not need*
> *to look back with sorrow on his past,*
> *for God gives him joy."*

I have come to realize, too, that to be content with a little is not a sign of low self-esteem. Rather, it is a testimony that man has an eye on a higher and more lasting thing in life, a thing that has un-diminishing value, a lasting quality, the true criterion of life's happiness.

"If I were a rich man ..." so the dairyman Tevye (in the movie *Fiddler on the Roof*) had dreamed. His dreaming was so ecstatic and a virtual reality that, for a few minutes, he forgot himself and all the hardship of life. But when the dreaming ended, he found his foot stuck in cow manure. Having viewed the movie many times over, however, I also had come to a realization and was moved by the fact that, deep inside, Tevye was a happy man. For he always managed to find goodness in nearly every man and meaning in every situation. He maintained courage and upright spirit to face the harsh reality of life, and continued to be the man his family could rely on, whatever the situation.

Pursuit of happiness? I believe its fulfillment should not be sought in any quantifiable things of this world but, instead, in contentment of the heart and peacefulness of the mind, where worries could not gnaw at your spirit and waste your body. Then, we will discover that not only the pursuit of happiness but also life and freedom will bring lasting and abundant fruition, wonderfully multiplied by many folds.

20

In Music There is
No East or West

Mike (an adopted English name) Shimizu, my roommate at the Southern Baptist Theological Seminary (Louisville KY, 1962-64) was a minister from Japan, about six years my senior. He was stout and jovial, with dimples on his cheeks when he smiled. Mike was on a sabbatical leave from his church, and was attending the seminary with a financial support from the Foreign Missions Board of the Southern Baptist Convention. His fellowship grants included travel, tuition and living stipends, while I was on my own *very* meager financial resources. From the very first week of the new school year, we found our cohabitation sharing a room in the dormitory beneficial in many ways. Besides being able to converse in our comfortable common language (Japanese), we also shared literally every expenditure item to make our ends meet, by putting into practice the wisdom of "two is cheaper than one." During the weekends when many students left the campus for recreational activities, we indulged in *our* form of relaxation and entertainment, which was to sit in our dormitory room and chitchat. Actually that was the only form of relaxation left for us, as we were financially short for any *paying* extracurricular activities. While we would talk about nearly every conceivable subject, our talk centered mostly on theology (his major field of study) and music (mine). It was during one of these weekend chats that *Pastor* Shimizu (there is no equivalent Asian term for *Reverend*) told me the following story:

Shortly after the end of the War, a performance of Handel's *Messiah* was publicized in Tokyo. The scheduled musical event aroused a tremendous excitement among the people in the city and the surrounding areas, Christians and non-Christians alike. For this was to be the very first full-scale performance of a Western masterpiece since the beginning of the War, complemented with a symphony orchestra, chorus and soloists. Long lines of people began to form the night before the concert, for fear of not being able to get in if showing up on the day of performance.

Finally the door was opened, and the people poured in; every space—seats and isles—was filled to absolute capacity of the large hall. The lights on the stage came on, and the scene was mesmerizing: the full chorus and orchestra was in their full array, and the soloists standing a mere few feet from the audience. Yet the auditorium, now with full capacity audience, was strangely quiet, but the air was intense, shivering with excitement of great anticipation.

Then, without warning, the lights went off, and the large concert hall, with all the people inside, was in total darkness. Immediately, there were commotions and a few cries, an eerie sense of fear that something awful might happen in that pitch black hall.

Then, as suddenly, from somewhere in the audience, someone started to sing:

> "*Kiyoshi kono yoru, Hoshi wa hikari*
> *Sukui no Miko wa, Mi-haha no mune ni*
> *Nemuri tamo(uh), Yume yasuku.*"

["Silent Night! Holy Night! All is calm, all is bright
'Round yon virgin mother and Child,
Holy Infant so tender and mild,
Sleep in heavenly peace, Sleep in heavenly
peace."]

Then, one by one, people began to join in the singing, and the voice began to swell as the verses were repeated over and over again. Soon the entire audience, in total darkness, became a massive chorus singing "Silent Night, Holy Night!" Eventually the lights returned, and the anticipated performance of *Messiah* went on without a hitch.

Mike Shimizu said, "*That* sensation of singing the simplest of hymn *Silent Night* in total darkness, with the memory of the terrible war and with horrendous human suffering but, now, in grateful restoration of peace over the land, was truly magical. One may say that it was perhaps greater than Handel's music. Perhaps, it was even God-sent."

Ah, the wonderful power of music; inexplicable, intoxicating, magical, memorable, and mesmerizing. And it is also universal. What is music? It is different sounds at different times to different people. It may be a soft voice of a mother's lullaby to her sucking babe resting on her breast, the sound of water to a thirsty throat, a gentle breeze to a traveler fatigued from journey, or a letter to a mother from her wandering son. Or it may be "Hi, daddy" from a child greeting a weary father after a long day's labor, or "Is it truly you?" of a voice on a long-distance telephone call between two long-lost friends. It does not need to be a voice of a coloratura, a melody played on a Stradivarius, or a symphonic poem performed by the Chicago Symphony Orchestra. It is a sound that delights a man's soul and lifts it to a realm beyond this mundane world.

Indeed, many things have been equated to music, and music is often regarded as the universal language. Music transcends ethnic and geographical boundaries, and it has been called the noblest of human arts. Tolstoy considered music as the most precious of man's creation, and said "Let Satan take away all man's creations, but only leave us music." Shakespeare even regarded music as the sign of man's virtue, saying,

> **"*The man that hath no music in himself* ...**
> is fit for treasons, stratagems, and spoils; ...
> *Let no such man be trusted*."**

A few years ago, I attended a music conference at Wuhan Conservatory (central China), and there was a presentation on the set of recently unearthed bone flutes, dated some nine thousand years old, before there was any writing of man. The presenter, a music archaeologist, showed a video in which a few scholars gave an *impromptu* "recital" on these bone flutes. The sound was delicate but the tones were amazingly clear and "in tune." While listening, I was seized by the realization that I was listening to the same musical sound that had delighted the people who had lived so many millennia ago. And I remembered reading *How Musical is Man* (University of Washington Press) by John Blacking, who boldly asserted that man was musical before lingual. As long as thirty-five thousand years ago, man was capable of making musical instruments that produced amazingly tuned tones; that was before man had developed facial muscles sufficient enough to articulate speech sounds. In other words, man was *intuitively* musical, that he needed music and created instruments of music before he needed words. One may be tempted to conclude, therefore, that one *innate* capacity that distinguished man from all other creatures on earth is that man is born with a *musical instinct*. And I secretly entertained the thought that it was this instinct that made me abandon my undergraduate training (in agricultural economics), and opt rather to pursue music, that musical inclination in me was a force stronger than any other interest of career pursuit.

According to my parents, I was a listless baby; I never seemed to want to sleep during the night. That posed a serious problem for my parents; my mother, the vice principal of an elementary school, was weary after her daily responsibility of administration and teaching, and my father also, with his ministerial duties that often required visitation of parishioners living a good distance from the church. The chore of wooing me to sleep fell on my father, who was frustrated that no amount of patting, wooing and rocking seemed to quiet me down to sleep. "Your father was angry," my mother had confided to me. "He said loudly that if you weren't his *first son*, he couldn't have cared, and would have let you cry all night long!"

In exasperation, my parents pleaded with my aunt, an elder sister of my father by three years, to come to take care of their nightly-crying son. My aunt, who had no children of her own, somehow discovered that this fussy baby would stop crying at the sound of singing. From then on, she would hold me and go to the living room, away from my parents' bedroom, and sing as she knocked at the thick wooden door, to the rhythm of an old Taiwanese folk evangelical hymn:

"*Goa-bin, pa-mng shi chi-tsui …?*"
["Who is he that knocks at the door?"]

"You were wooed to sleep every night by the voice of your aunt singing and the sound of her knocking at the door," my parents had told me many times.

My aunt went back home after about six months, when my nightly sleep had become normally regular. Then my parents bought an Edison *VOICE OF THE MASTER* gramophone, the very first in our small mining town, and I was wooed to sleep by the music from the 78*rpm* records on the Edison machine. I was told that I began to learn to crank the machine when I was about four years old, but inevitably would fuss and cry when the gramophone stopped playing, because I was not big enough to crank up the machine to play the music to the end. Subsequently, I had succeeded in breaking the only gramophone in the town before I entered elementary school.

It was many years afterward, when I was already in junior high, that my aunt came from the east coast of Taiwan to visit us on the north coast, and I can still remember that day. She smiled broadly and called me *A-shiong*, my childhood name, and posing a gesture of holding a baby in her left arm and knocking with her right fist, began to sing "*Goa-bin, pa-mng, shi chi-tsui ...?*" (Her singing voice was gentle and with a sweet lilt, but was quite out of tune.) Then, still beaming, she asked in Taiwanese *ho-loh* dialect, "*E ki-eh, boh?*" ("Do you still remember?")

At the Japanese primary school, Mrs. Mori, my first-grade teacher, recognized my singing and, to my childish chagrin, I was put on stage on the field-day program to sing and dance with the girls (while the boys performed sword dances without the girls). In the third grade, Miss Yoshino, my homeroom teacher fresh out of *normal* high school (senior-high level teacher-training school) introduced to the school a new music activity, a musical game of sort. First, students were all asked to stand up, with eyes closed and right hands raised high. Then the teacher will play various chords on the portable pump organ, and students were asked to identify the chords by numbers, one finger for chord "one," two fingers for chord "two," and so on. After playing each chord, the teacher would announce the correct answer, and those with the wrong number of fingers out would have to sit down. The game, or drill, was a sort of "harmonic recognition," what in the college curriculum today is called "harmonic dictation" but without any theoretical connotation. There, DO-MI-SOL was simply called "chord one," DO-FA-LA as "chord two," TI-RE-SOL as "chord three," RE-SOL-TI as "chord four," and MI-SOL-DO as "chord five." And the game would continue in this fashion until no student remained standing; then a new round of the game would begin.

Somehow, almost from day one, I was able to identify every chord correctly. I suppose harmony was as natural to me as the air I breathed, since I grew up in the church listening to hymns. After a while Miss Yoshino (still living, in northern Japan, in the district of Yoshida, the ancestral land of her late husband's feudal lineage) became curious and, as I was always the only one left standing at every round of this musical game, she would intentionally play some "wrong" chords, just trying to throw me off. Then I would close my fist tight, to signal that those were not among the five chords to be identified.

Game after game, week after week, I would be the only one standing in the harmonic drill game, and "this *bespeckled* boy who could never miss a chord" became a school-wide oddity, and other teachers and even the principal, Mr. Torikai, a severe military man who reigned over the elementary school as if it were a military camp, came, out of disbelief, to observe this kid "*mimi ga aru*" ("with an ear"). The boy who, until then, was not among the popular (I was not good in PE, and nearly always came in last in the race, and I couldn't even fight well, losing both of the two fist fights in my entire life), was now suddenly acknowledged even by elder schoolmates. My boy classmates encouraged me: "You are nearsighted and could never be a fighting soldier. But you could become a submariner, and listen to the sound of enemy ships." And I felt proud that now I would someday be able to serve the Emperor.

During my high school years, too, the music teachers recognized my musical ability and, as far as I know, I was until then the only student ever appointed assistant conductor to the all-boy choir (high schools in Taiwan were not coeducational). In college, I was the most junior ever (at the end of my sophomore year) to be elected the glee club conductor. I immediately started to "reform" the glee club membership, changing it from an all-male chorus to a mixed-voice musical organization. Without any formal training, I tried to take down music from listening to 78rpm recordings (Western music scores were scarce in those days), and even tried my hand at arranging music, and organized and conducted the entire concert program once every semester. After graduation and coming to the United States, changing my major field of study to music seemed only natural. And, for the two master's degrees, I fool heartedly triple- and double-majored in voice, conducting, and composition. I guess I was a bit overzealous; I was just trying to catch up with the lost years.

One day during my second year of doctoral study at Northwestern University, I was summoned to the dean's office, in response to an urgent call from one of the chief editors at Summy Birchard Music Company (Evanston, IL). On the phone I was told that Mr. Shinichiro Suzuki, the founder of the world-renown *Suzuki violin method* and an eminent educator, was visiting the company headquarters at its invitation. Since Mr. Suzuki spoke little English (and Summy Birchard did not have anyone on the staff fluent in Japanese), they needed an interpreter, someone who was fully bilingual and also knowledgeable in music. I was immediately chauffeured from the NU Music School building (nicknamed the "white elephant," an ugly pre-World War II structure painted white) to the sparkling company headquarters office, and was introduced to the grand old man of music. I accompanied him for the next two days, helping both parties on matters relating to edition and issuing of Mr. Suzuki's violin-method publications.

Mr. Suzuki was already in his seventies, very short in stature but spritely in spirit and jovial in his demeanor. In an interview with reporters, he was asked to speak on his philosophy of music, and I realized that he was also a philosopher. Not only did he believe in the universality of musical language, but also in the power of music's to instill lasting influence in nurturing a wholesome character in all children.

> "Music is the *mother tongue* of all children in the world.
> Music learning is the most natural of all learning activities.
> Music instills in children a sense of beauty and harmony, and musical activity not only gives children a sense of personal achievement, but also teaches them the spirit of cooperation and the value of team effort.
> Music is in the heart of every living person.
> I also believe that, through music, we can hope to bring peace to this world.
> No other art can enjoin all human beings in true harmony.
> I hope the United Nations would recognize this."

His statements were short but concise, and I thought I had never heard a more eloquent and convincing testimonial of the value and the magical power of music for mankind.

Actually, the United Nations did recognize the value of music, and I believe Mr. Suzuki certainly knew this. Under UNESCO, an organization was created to study and explore the music of all the people in the world. This organization is the International Council for Traditional Music (ICTM), with headquarters at the University of California at Los Angeles. However, it has become an institution unto itself, dedicated more for the promotion of *academic* activity on "world music" (known in academic circles as *ethnomusicology*). With this orientation, every year a group of "musical culture scientists"—the *ethnomusicologists* who earlier were called *comparative music scientists*—gets together in an exotic land to read to one another scholarly papers and research reports. In this organization—the original purpose of which was to cultivate and broaden channels of human understanding through music—the *mother tongue of all mankind* was rarely promoted. Instead, the focus and purpose of the organization's activity seem less than broadly subscribed, and there is really not that much dialogue even among its members. I have yet to see any tangible evidence of the work of this organization that has promoted understanding and communication among different people, except perhaps some cultivation of collegiality with their foreign colleagues—the fellow comparative musical scientists whose very professional label tends to conjure in the mind of the outsiders a sense of awe but always from a respectable distance. And I know of several ethnomusicologists who could not even *sing* the music about which they claim to be expert and have devoted their study. In other words, they are, as Shakespeare said, "*The men that hath no music in himself.*" Somehow, I don't think that was exactly what Mr. Suzuki had in mind.

Traveling in China, I have heard Mongolian songs of the northern Asian steppes and mountain songs of China's southern provinces, the full-chest "head"-voice of young men and women, their singing free and soaring high into the open and cloudless skies. I also have heard the songs of minority nationals living in isolated mountain villages of Guangxi and Yunnan provinces; utterly simple songs consisting of no more than five notes that are repeated over and over, sung to lyrics that were composed spontaneously but always from their innocent and untarnished heart.

I once brought a dozen or so of my American students for a field study trip up in a tiny village, consisting only of a handful of huts, a few thousand feet above sea level, above the clouds. This remote village in Guangxi Province was accessible only by walking the narrow muddy roads snaking through the "dragon-rib" rice paddies carved out on steep mountain terrains. Entering the mayor's house, the largest in the village, we sat down on low wooden stools, barely eight or so inches high, and listened to several old ladies in their sixties and seventies singing their impromptu songs. We were told that these songs were a form of speech, and the women would make up lyrics and improvise the music as they sang. We also were served herb tea and gruel of some indescribable grains. When we were saying good-byes, these ladies sent us off at their door steps, lingeringly shaking our hands and repeating again and again, "Do come back to see us" and sang another impro-vised song of farewell. We knew in our heart that we would most likely never see them again but, at the same time, felt that their voices would remain ringing in our hearts' ears. Masterpiece of music they certainly are not. But what is a masterpiece of music? Their music utterly inno-cent, yet profoundly moving singing is equal to any that has ever been composed by man.

In ancient times, in all early civilizations, men of wisdom—they were called philosophers—believed that music affected not only our hearts and souls but also the state of the cosmos, and that music was the only language through which man could commune with the gods. As late as the eighteenth century, philosophers, scientists and mathe-maticians—among them the great astronomer Johannes Kepler—believed in this, and theory of music (then called *harmony*) was a required subject in all university curricula, collectively referred to as the *quadrivium* (the *"way of the four"* subjects in the inquiry of truth; the term was coined by Boethius, early sixth century Roman and the last of the Greek philosophers). And anyone who claimed to be edu-cated was expected to be conversant in the four subjects of *mathemat-*

ics, astronomy (or astrology), *geometry,* and *harmony* (music theory). Why these four, and these four only, for a man to study to be regarded as wise? Because these four subjects required the knowledge of numbers, and number was believed to be the language of the gods. For god created heaven and earth with the wisdom of numbers (hence the Sumerian mythology of god creating the heaven and earth in "six" days; *cf.* **[III]**, on *"Numerology"*).

We the modern man no longer believe in such hocus-pocus. But, then, as we trust our eyes and pen-and-paper way of reasoning and less on our hearts and intuitions, we may be missing a glimpse or two into what the ancient wise men had seen, such as in the power and effect of music. Maybe there is a far greater power and magic in music than we give credit for. Of course, when we jump up and down and twist and twirl to the incessant, blaring and ear-splitting beats of percussion and to the deafening volume of singing and yelling, we tend NOT to listen to that still small voice in music that speaks more directly to our heart.

There was a commercial many decades ago that had a wonderful song lyric:

> *"I'd want to teach the world to sing in perfect harmony;*
> *I'd like to hold it in my arms, and keep it company.*
> *I'd like to see the world for once all standing hand in hand,*
> *And hear them echo through the hills,*
> *'Ah, peace throughout the land.'"*

Perfect *harmony?* I believe it is NOT in reference to the learned academic subject of "theory of harmony" engaged in the study of analytical masterpieces of Bach, Beethoven, and Brahms. Rather, it is about the quality of music; it is about the natural *sympathetic* response of man's heart and soul to the sounds of music, however simple that music may be. To be "in harmony" means to be *in tune*, in *concordant reverberation*, in *rational* and *natural* synch with the things surrounding us. We may refer to the original meaning of the word *symphony* (*sin-*, *syn-*, or, earlier, *sum-*, or *sym*, as in *syn*chronize and *sym*pathetic, plus *phonia* or *phono*, as in *phono*graph and *phone*tic), which was to "*sound* [together] *as one.*

If music is in all of us, and if we are an unique creature because we alone are capable of making music and enjoy listening to it, and to find in it incomparable beauty, joy, and comfort, then man is capable of creating a *universal symphony* that will resound when we are in *harmony with* all others. It is then that we will be able to shout altogether, "*Peace and Harmony throughout the land.*"

Music binds all mankind. Music is Man, and Man is Music. And, in music, there is no East or West.

A Very Selectively Short Bibliography A, B (and small) c

Asimov, Isaac.
  Asimov on Numbers (Pocket Books; Simon & Schuster).

  Asimov on the Bible (Simon & Schuster).

Boorstin, Daniel J.
  The Creators (Vintage; Random House).

  The Discoverers (Vintage; Random House).

Cho, Gene J.
  The Discovery of Musical Equal Temperament in China and Europe in the Sixteenth Century (Edwin Mellen Press).

  The Replica of the Ark of the Covenant in Japan: The Mystery of MiFune-Shiro (iUniverse; Barnes and Noble).

978-0-595-47443-1
0-595-47443-8

www.ingramcontent.com/pod-product-compliance
Lightning Source LLC
Chambersburg PA
CBHW030301290526
45785CB00001B/177